Easy Piano

Taylor Swift
Midnights

ISBN 978-1-70518-463-4

Visit Hal Leonard Online at
www.halleonard.com

World headquarters, contact:
Hal Leonard
7777 West Bluemound Road
Milwaukee, WI 53213
Email: info@halleonard.com

In Europe, contact:
Hal Leonard Europe Limited
1 Red Place
London, W1K 6PL
Email: info@halleonardeurope.com

In Australia, contact:
Hal Leonard Australia Pty. Ltd.
4 Lentara Court
Cheltenham, Victoria, 3192 Australia
Email: info@halleonard.com.au

LAVENDER HAZE

Words and Music by TAYLOR SWIFT,
JACK ANTONOFF, MARK ANTHONY SPEARS,
JAHAAN AKIL SWEET, SAM DEW
and ZOË KRAVITZ

much. _____ And

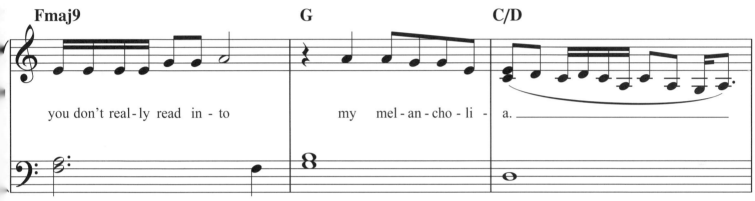

you don't real-ly read in-to my mel-an-cho-li - a. _____

I been un-der scru-ti - ny. Yeah, oh

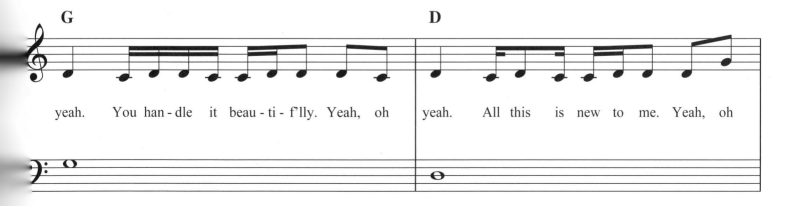

yeah. You han-dle it beau-ti-f'lly. Yeah, oh yeah. All this is new to me. Yeah, oh

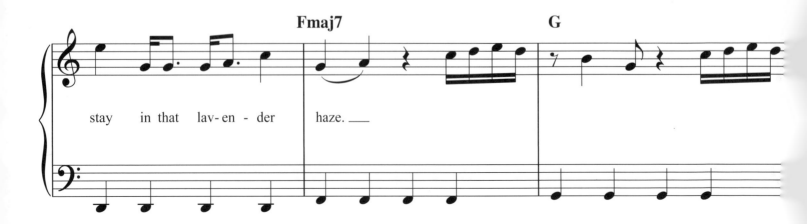

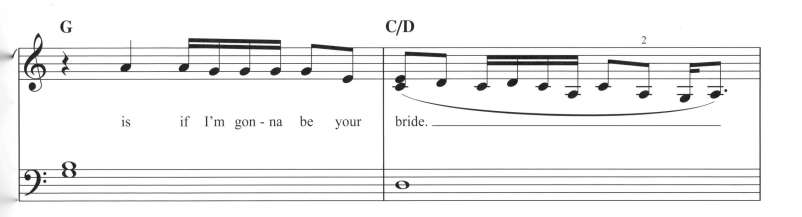

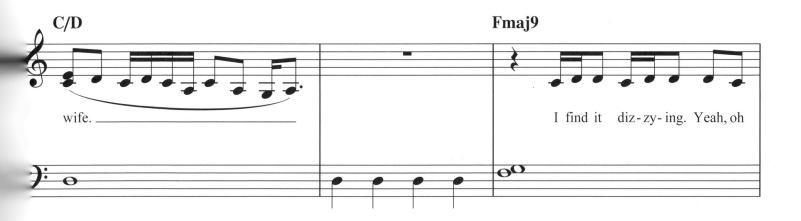

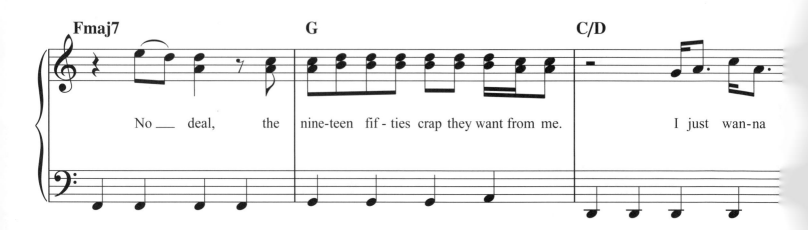

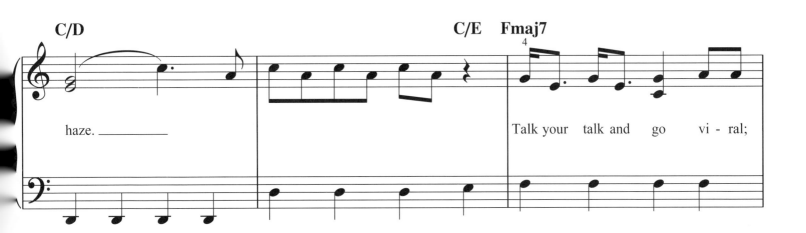

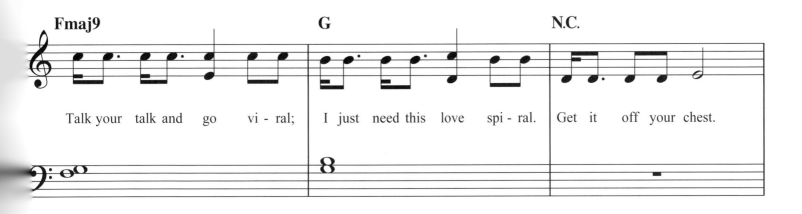

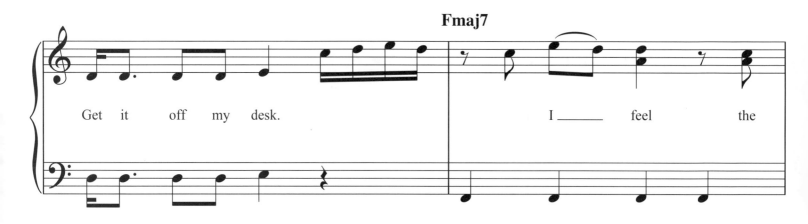

Fmaj7

Get it off my desk. I _____ feel the

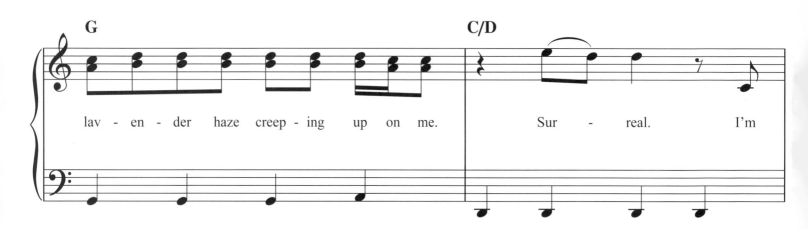

G   **C/D**

lav - en - der haze creep - ing up on me.   Sur - real. I'm

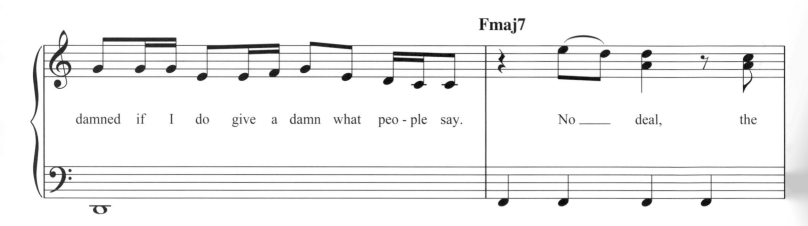

Fmaj7

damned if I do give a damn what peo - ple say.   No _____ deal, the

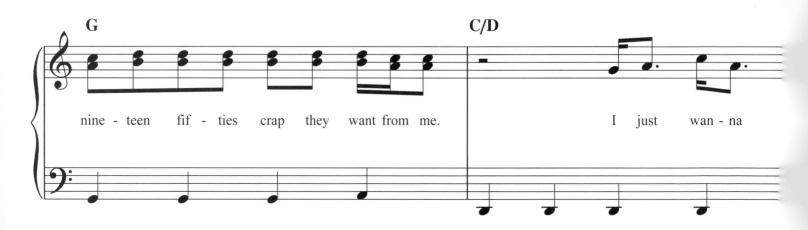

G   **C/D**

nine - teen fif - ties crap they want from me.   I just wan - na

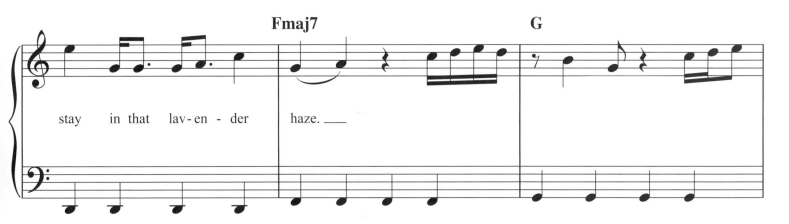

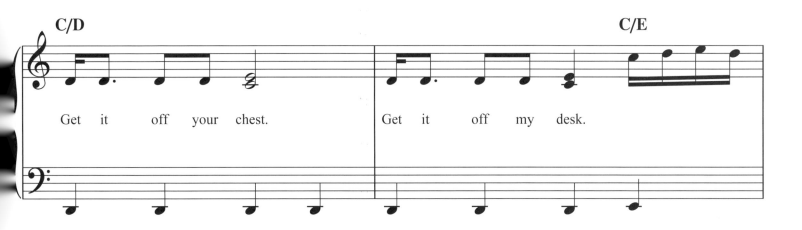

MAROON

Words and Music by TAYLOR SWIFT
and JACK ANTONOFF

Moderately slow, in 2

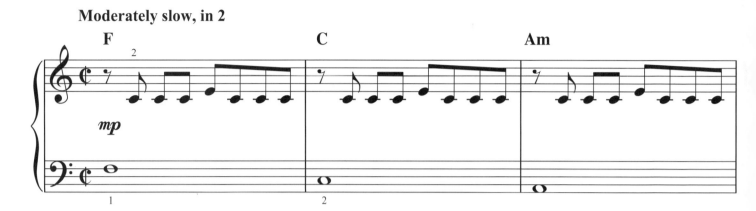

When the morn-ing came we were clean-ing in-cense off your

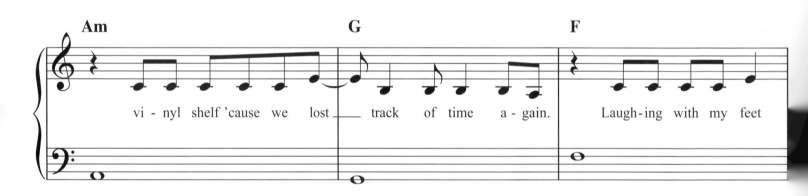

vi-nyl shelf 'cause we lost track of time a-gain. Laugh-ing with my feet

in your lap, like you were my clos-est friend.

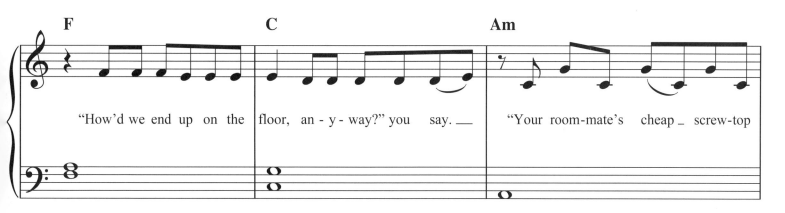

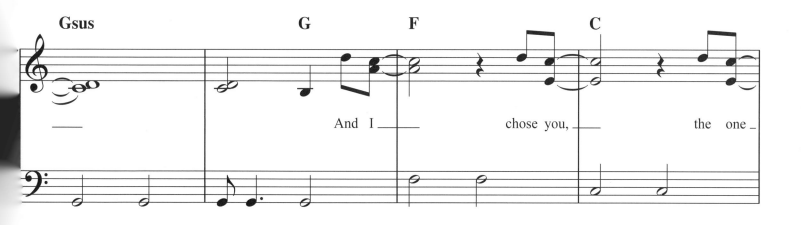

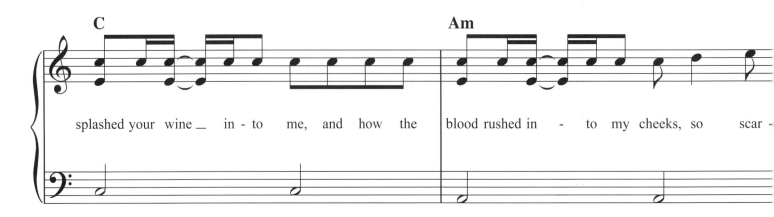

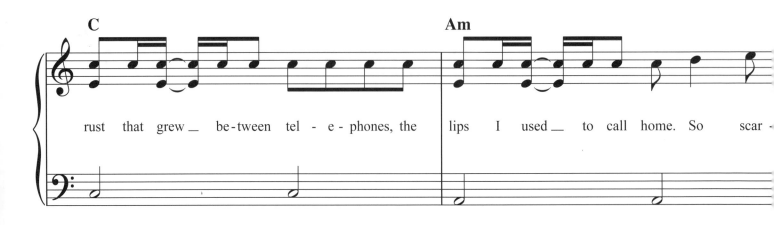

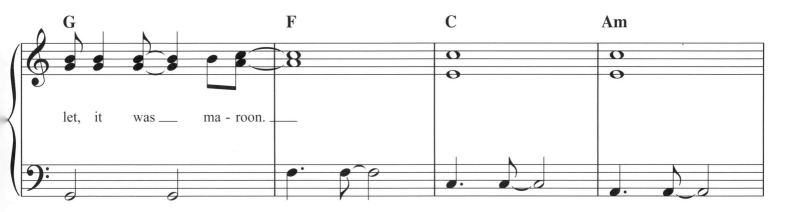

let, it was ma - roon.

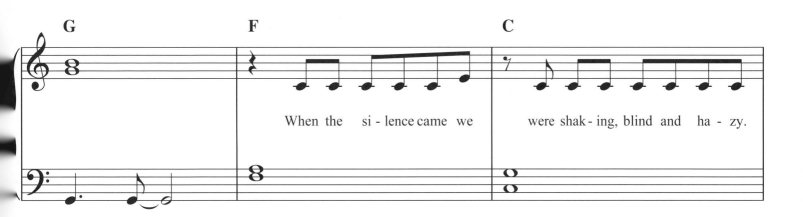

When the si - lence came we were shak - ing, blind and ha - zy.

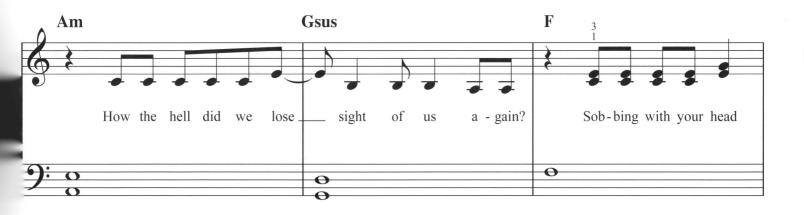

How the hell did we lose sight of us a - gain? Sob - bing with your head

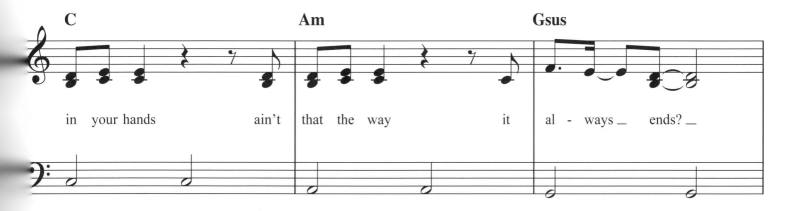

in your hands ain't that the way it al - ways ends?

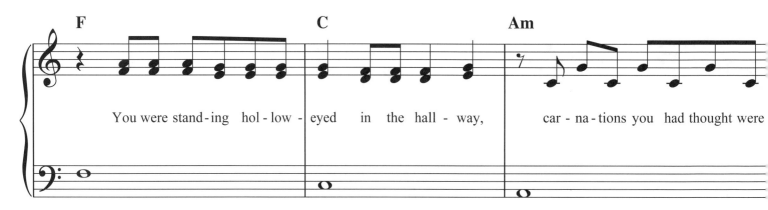

15

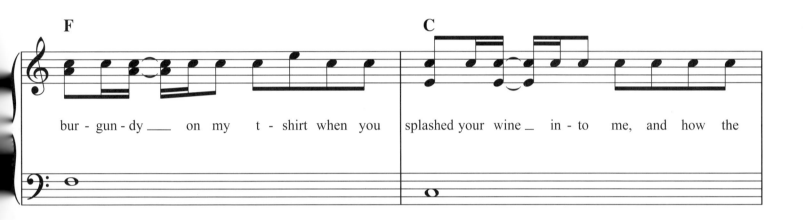

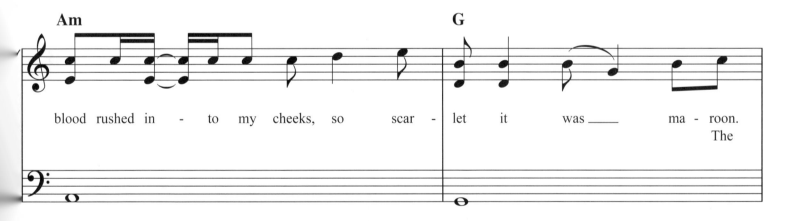

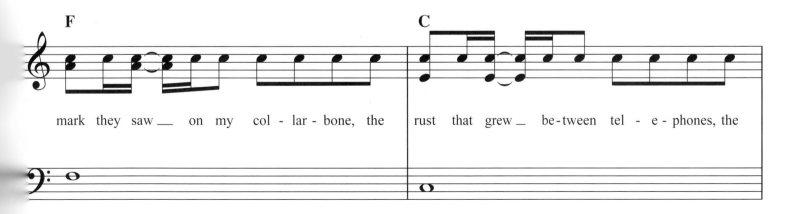

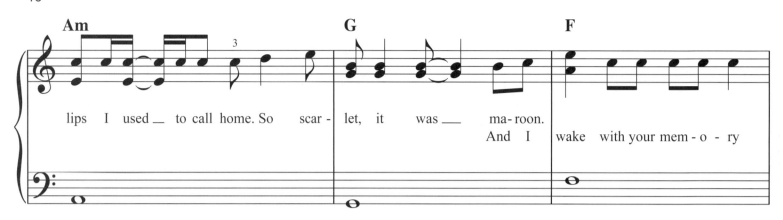

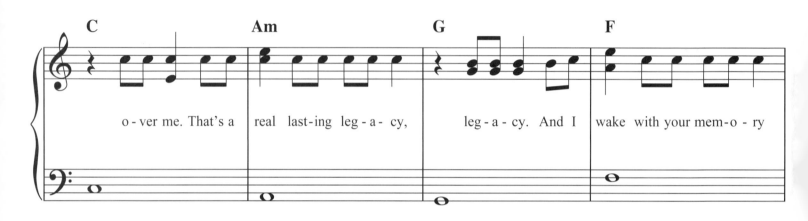

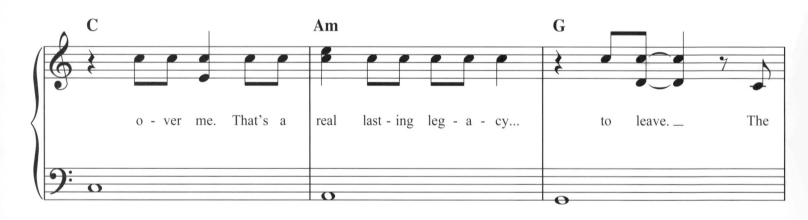

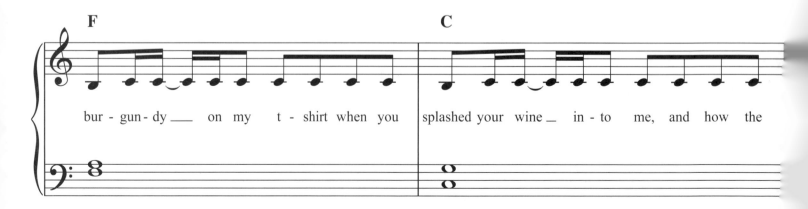

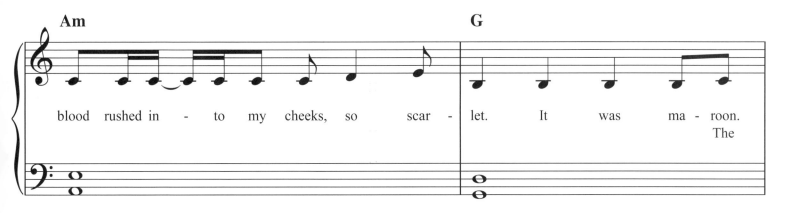

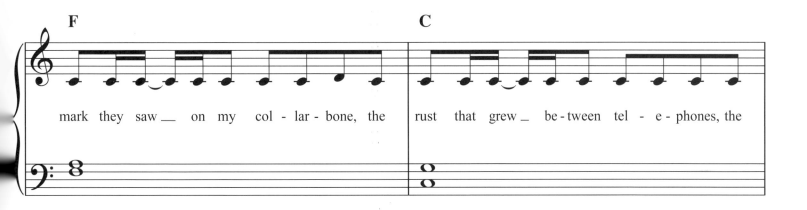

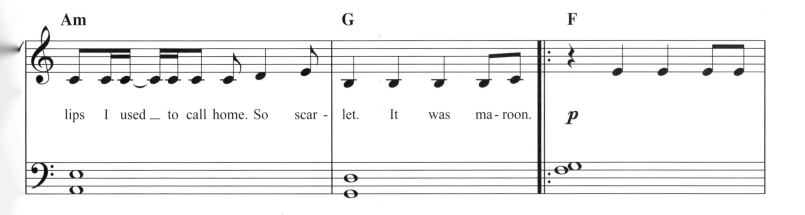

ANTI-HERO

Words and Music by TAYLOR SWIFT
and JACK ANTONOFF

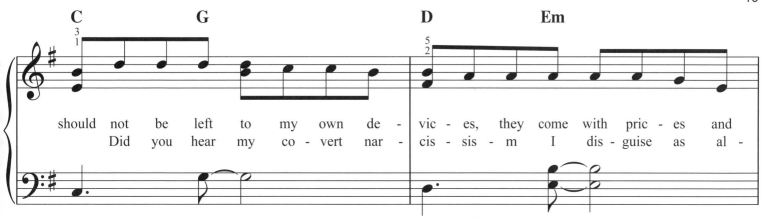

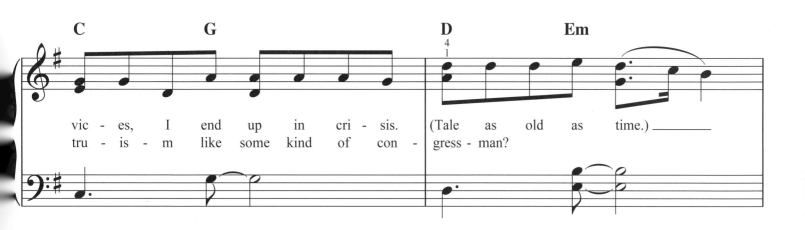

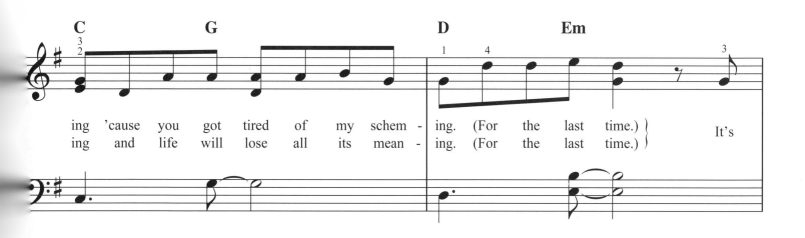

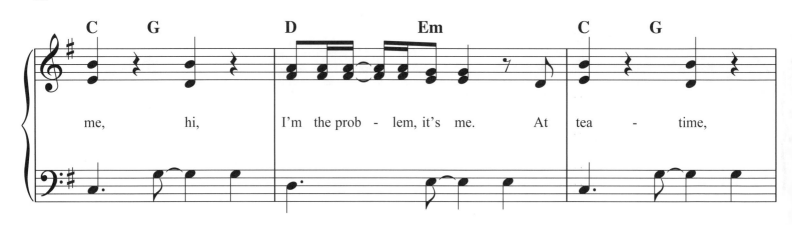

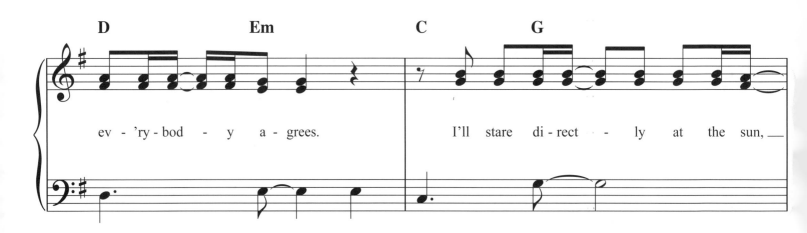

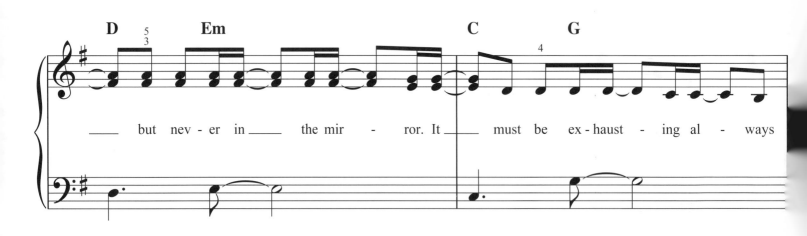

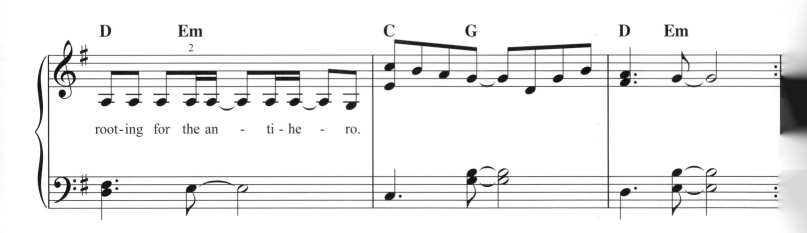

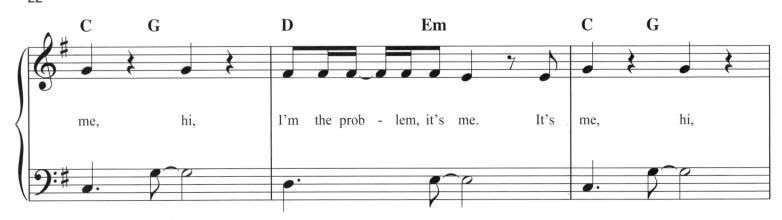

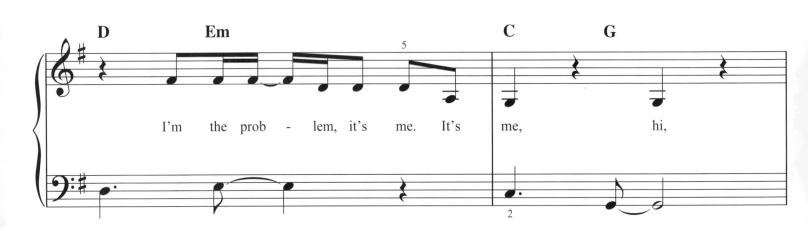

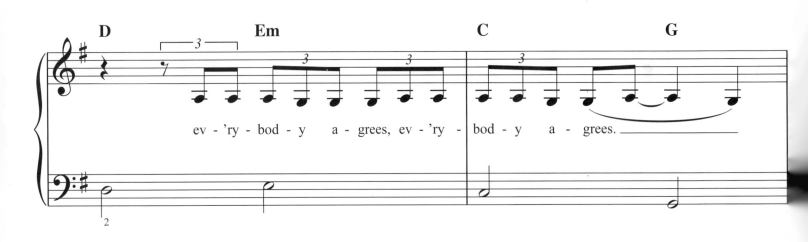

I'm the prob - lem, it's me. At tea - time,

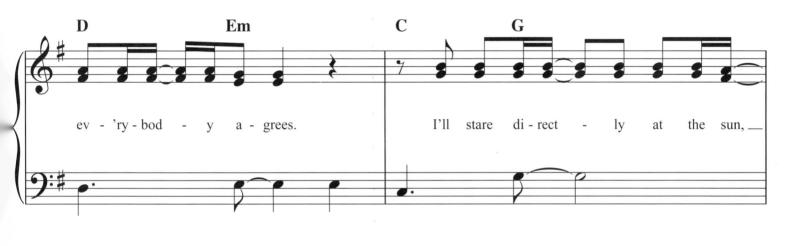

ev - 'ry - bod - y a - grees. I'll stare di - rect - ly at the sun, ___

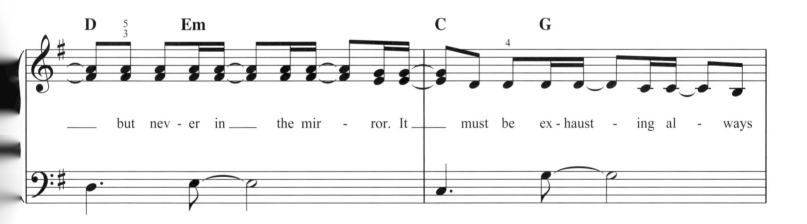

___ but nev - er in ___ the mir - ror. It ___ must be ex - haust - ing al - ways

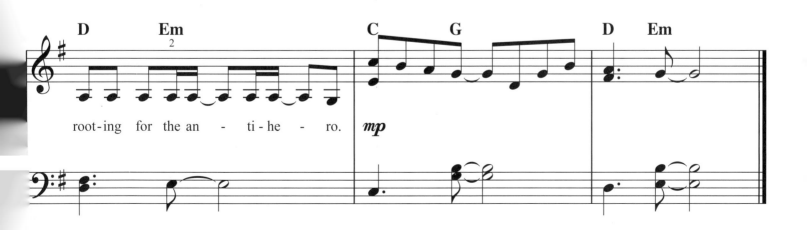

root - ing for the an - ti - he - ro. *mp*

SNOW ON THE BEACH

Words and Music by TAYLOR SWIFT,
ELIZABETH GRANT and JACK ANTONOFF

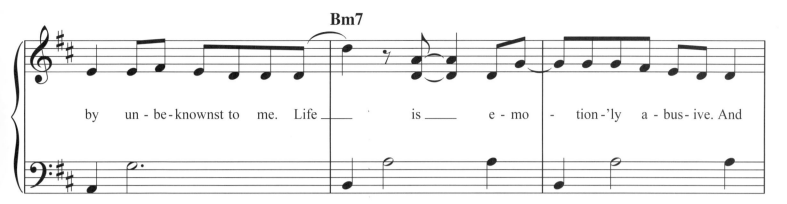

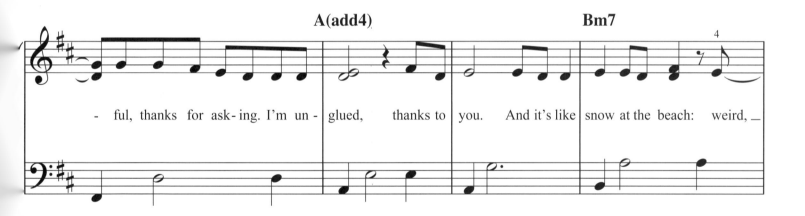

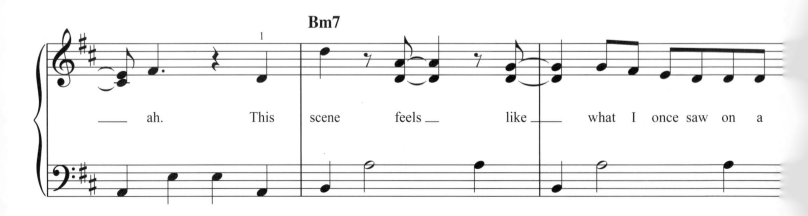

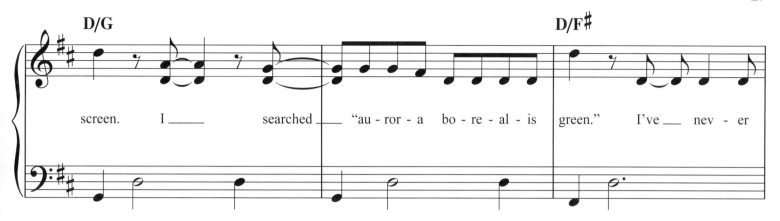

screen. I ____ searched ____ "au - ror - a bo - re - al - is green." I've ___ nev - er

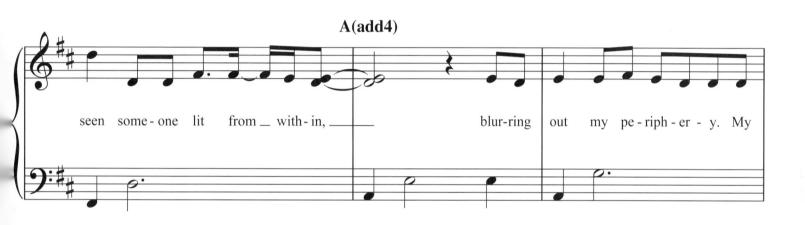

seen some - one lit from ___ with - in, ____ blur - ring out my pe - riph - er - y. My

smile is ____ like ____ I won a con - test, and to hide that ___ would ___

___ be so dis - hon - est. And it's fine to ____ fake ___ it 'til you make it. 'Til you

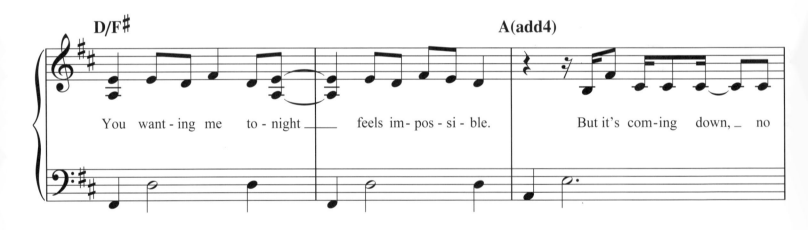

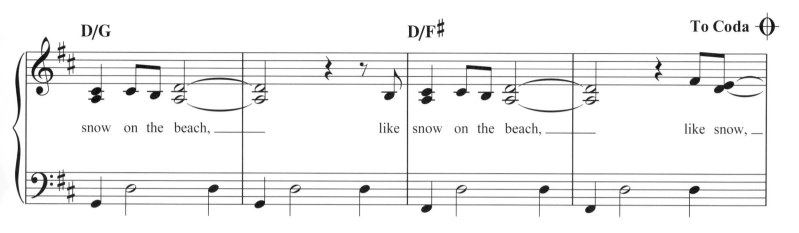

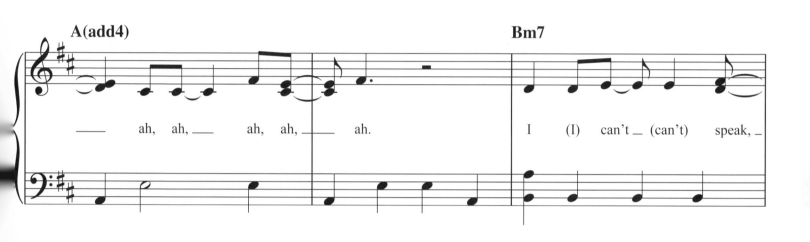

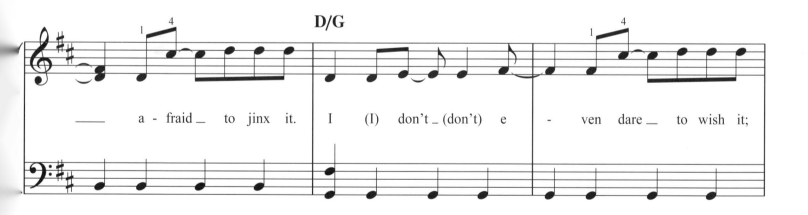

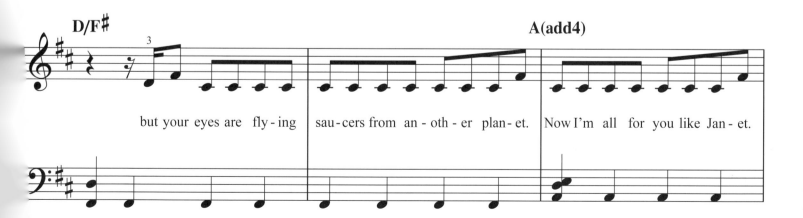

N.C.

D.S. al Coda

Can this be a real thing? Can it?

Are we fall-ing like __

CODA

A(add4)

__ but it's com-ing down, __ no sound, it's all a-round. It's

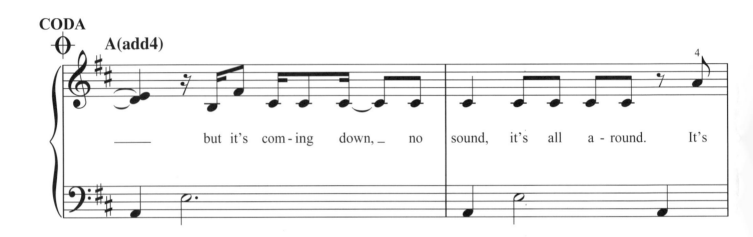

Bm7

com-ing down, __ it's com-ing down, __ it's com-ing down, __ it's com-ing down. __

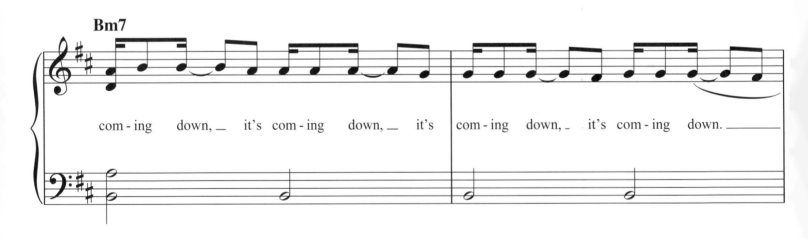

D/G

D/F#

__ (Like snow on the beach.) It's com-ing down, __ it's com-ing down, __ it's

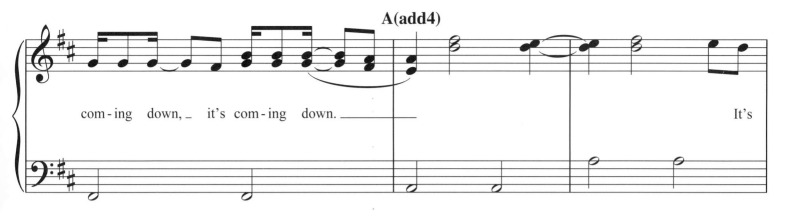

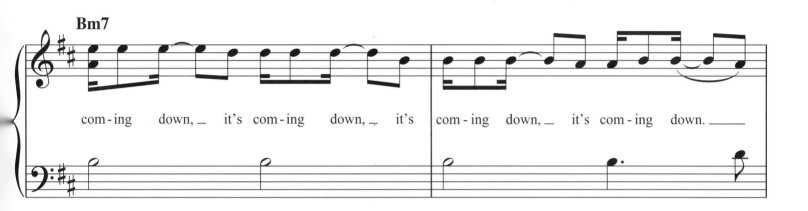

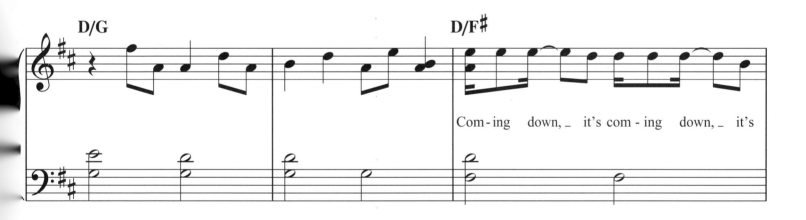

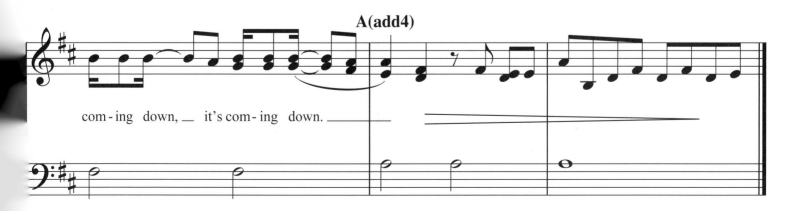

YOU'RE ON YOUR OWN, KID

Words and Music by TAYLOR SWIFT
and JACK ANTONOFF

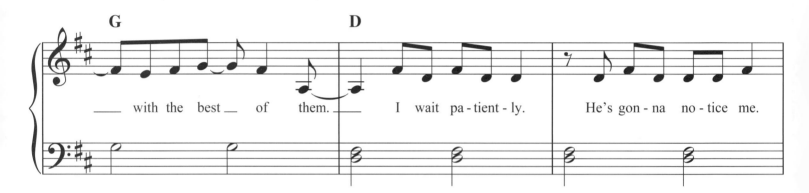

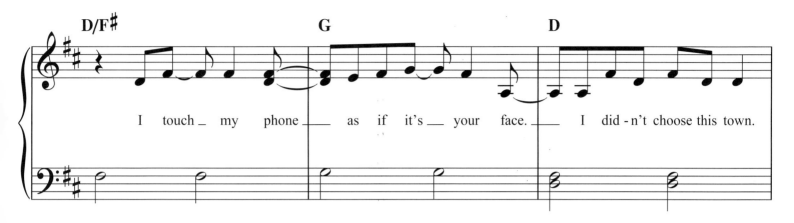

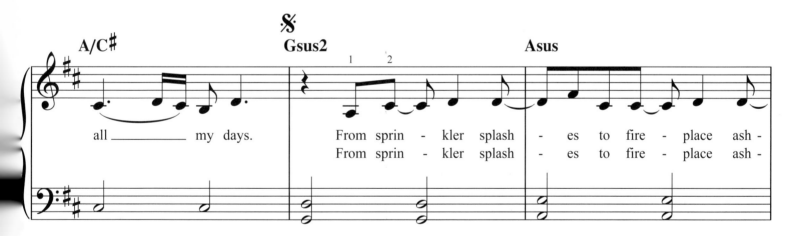

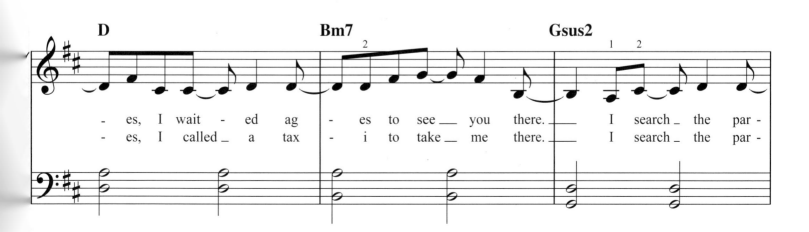

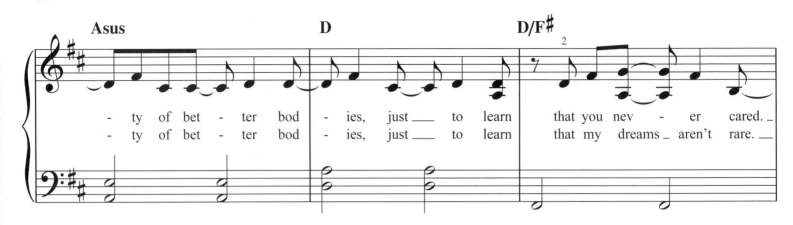

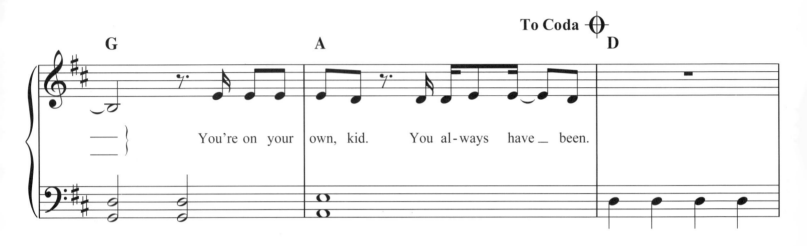

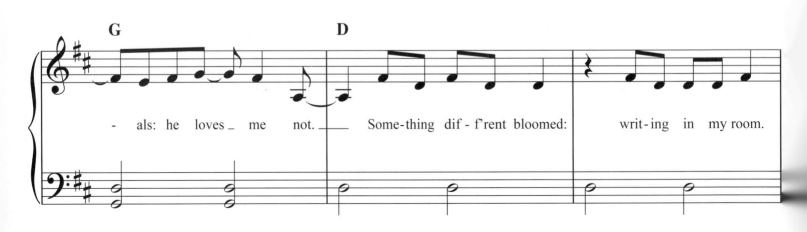

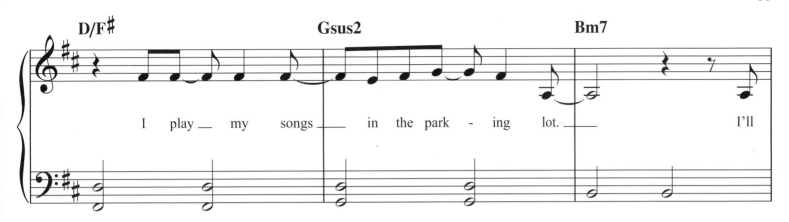

I play __ my songs __ in the park - ing lot. __ I'll

run __ a - way.

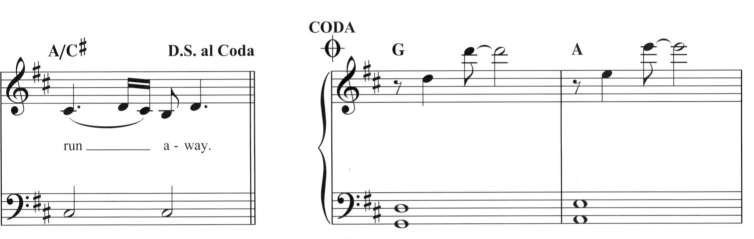

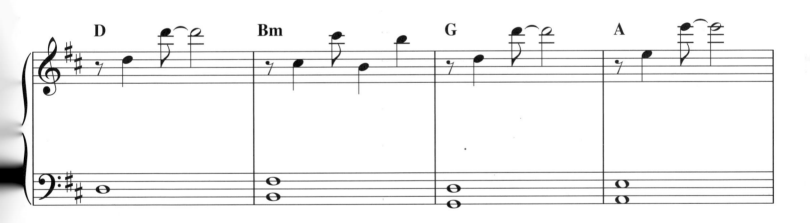

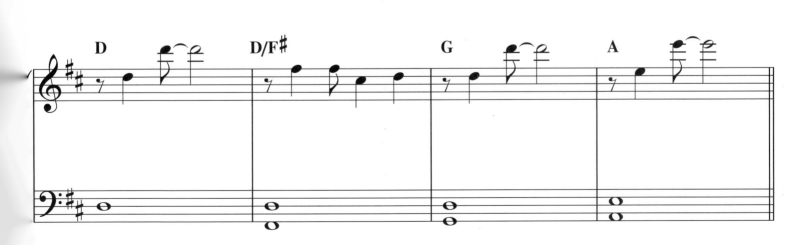

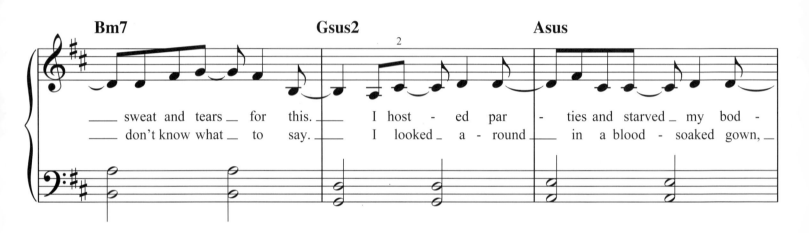

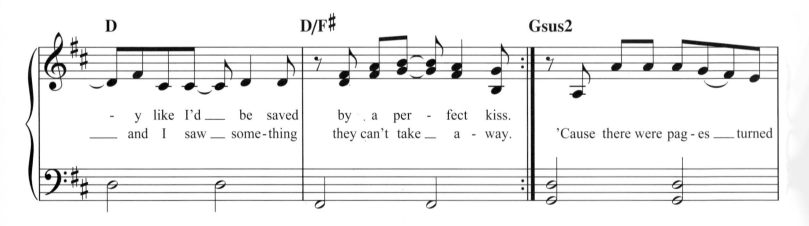

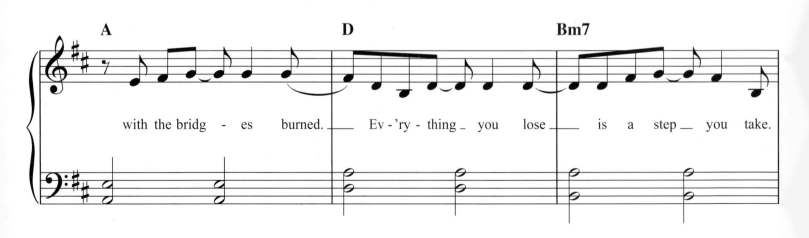

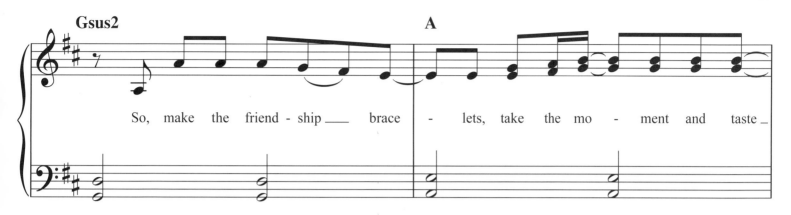

So, make the friend-ship ___ brace - lets, take the mo - ment and taste ___

___ it. You've got ___ no rea - son to be ___ a - fraid. ___ You're on your own, ___

___ kid. Yeah, you can face ___ this.

You're on your own, ___ kid. ___ You al - ways have ___ been. ___

KARMA

Words and Music by TAYLOR SWIFT,
JACK ANTONOFF, MARK ANTHONY SPEARS,
KEANU TORRES and JAHAAN AKIL SWEET

Moderate Pop

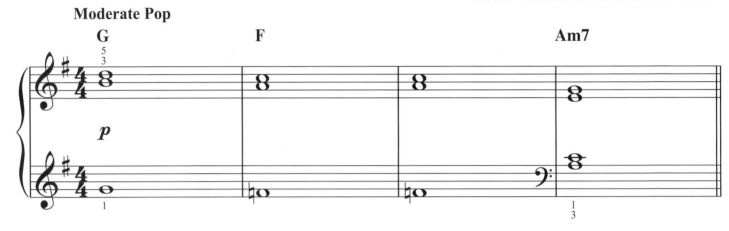

You're talk-ing trash for the hell of it, ad-dic-ted to be-tray-al but you're rel-e-vant.

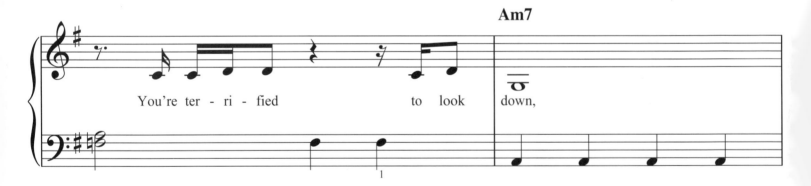

You're ter-ri-fied to look down, 'cause if you dare,

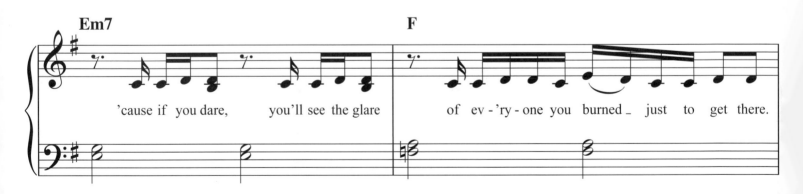

'cause if you dare, you'll see the glare of ev-'ry-one you burned _ just to get there.

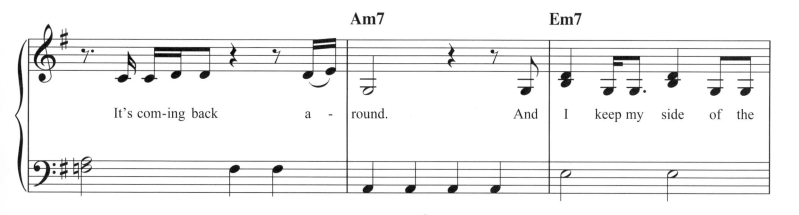

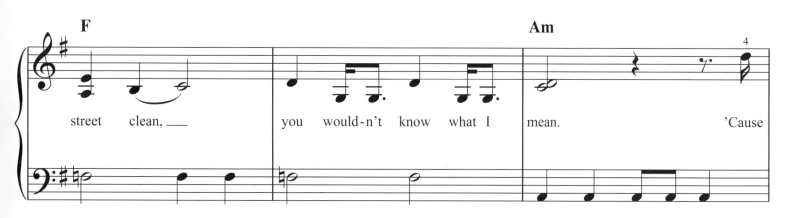

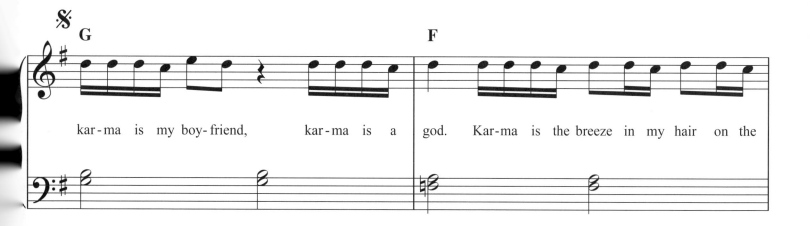

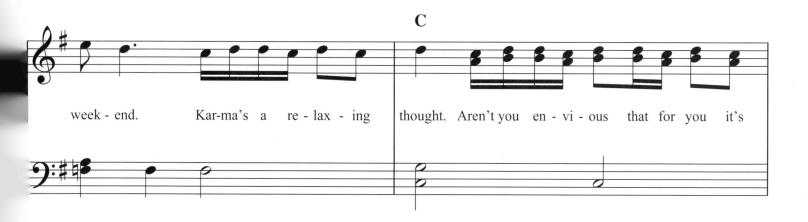

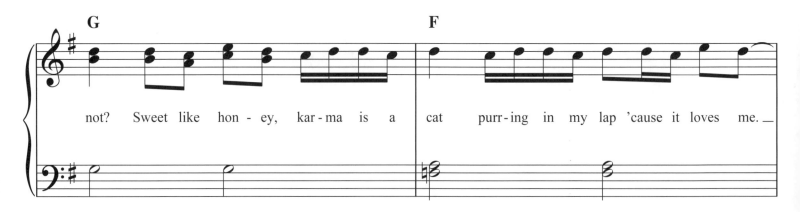

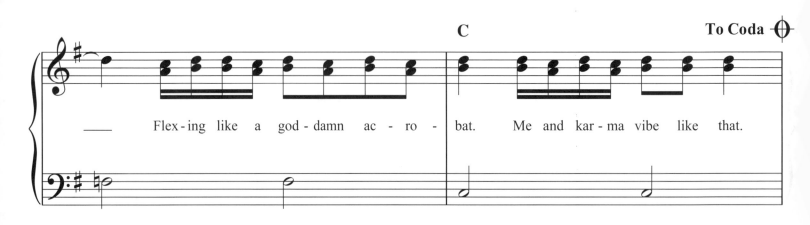

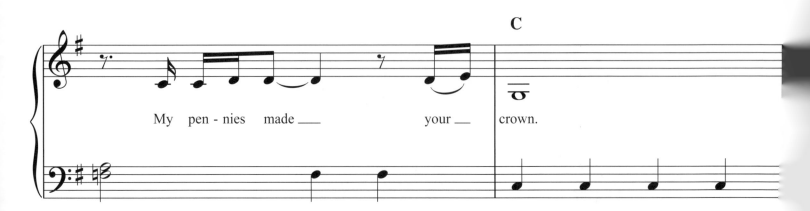

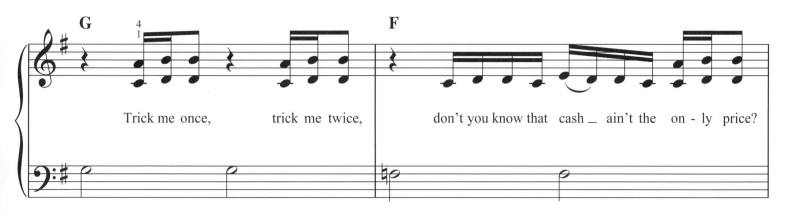

Trick me once, trick me twice, don't you know that cash _ ain't the on - ly price?

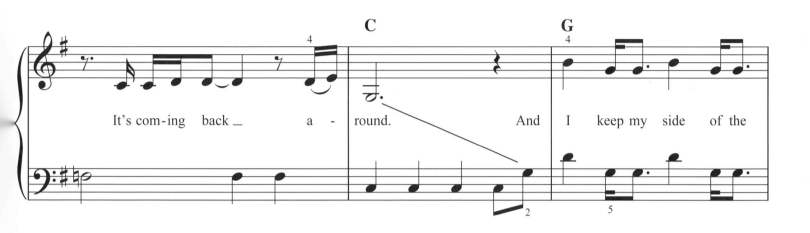

It's com-ing back _ a - round. And I keep my side of the

street clean. _ You would-n't know what I mean. 'Cause

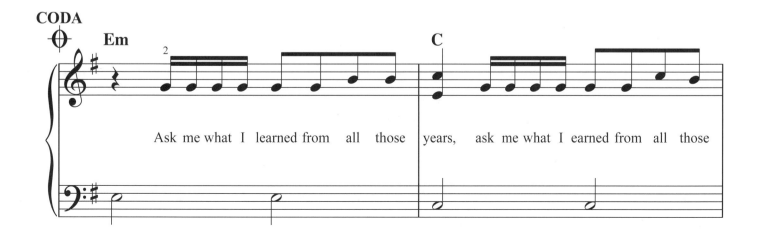

Ask me what I learned from all those years, ask me what I earned from all those

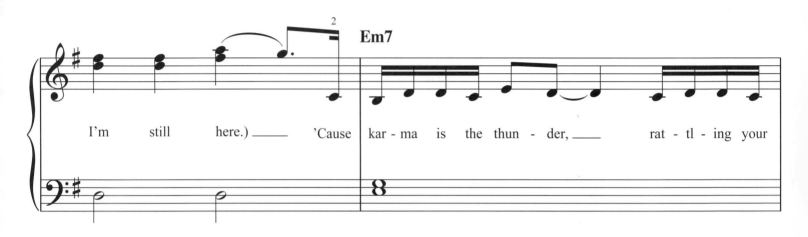

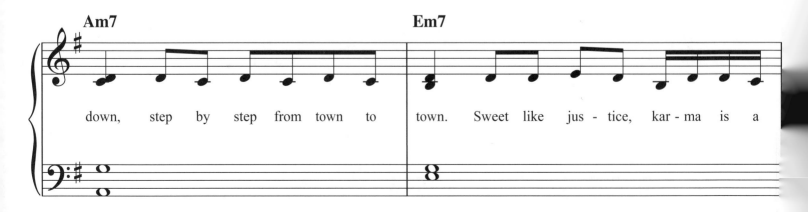

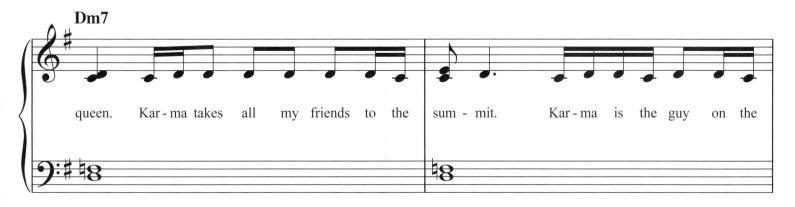

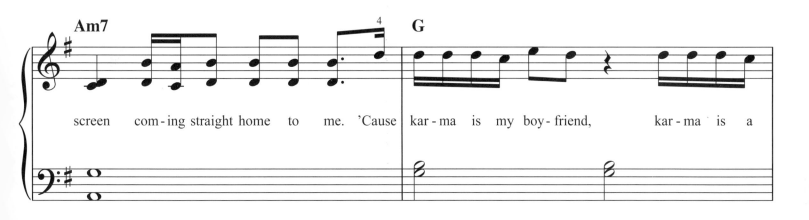

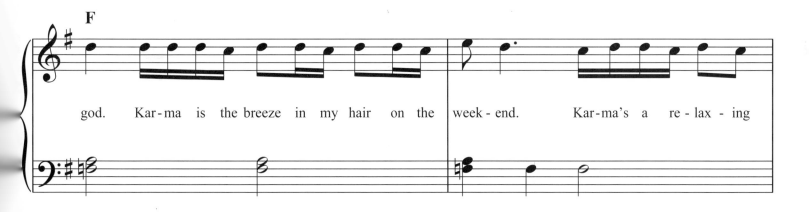

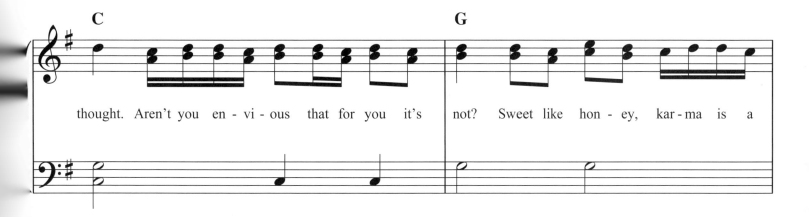

cat purr-ing in my lap 'cause it loves me.____ Flex-ing like a god-damn ac-ro-

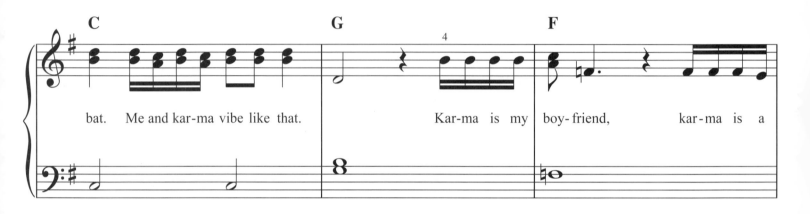

bat. Me and kar-ma vibe like that. Kar-ma is my boy-friend, kar-ma is a

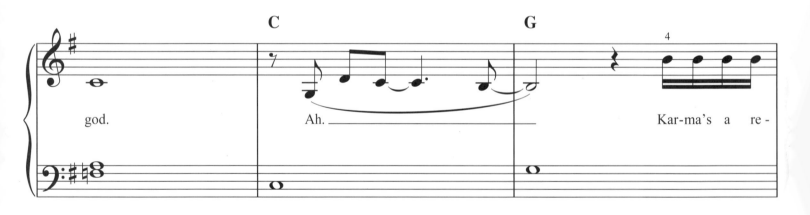

god. Ah._____ Kar-ma's a re-

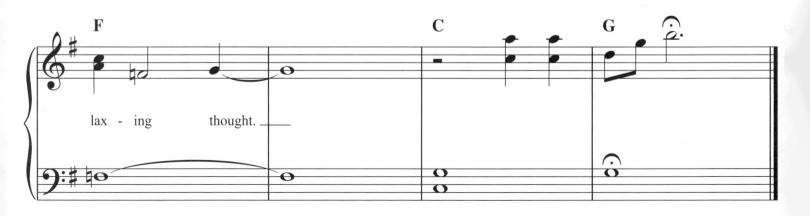

lax - ing thought.____

MASTERMIND

Words and Music by TAYLOR SWIFT
and JACK ANTONOFF

Moderately fast

mf Once up-on a time the plan-ets and the fates and

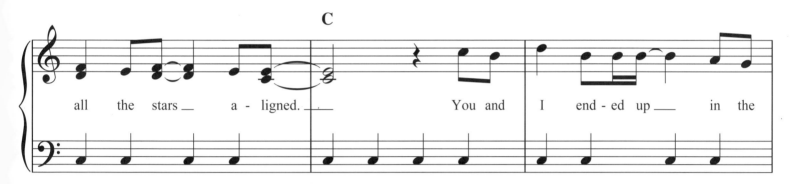

all the stars a - ligned. You and I end-ed up __ in the

same room at the same time, __ and the touch __

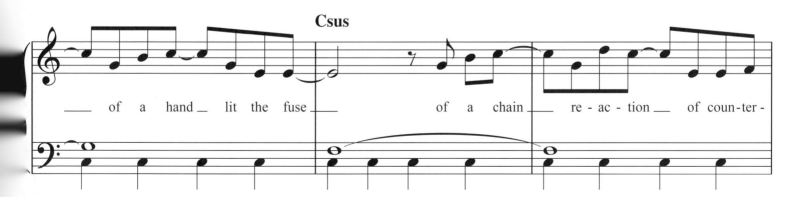

__ of a hand __ lit the fuse __ of a chain __ re - ac - tion __ of coun-ter-

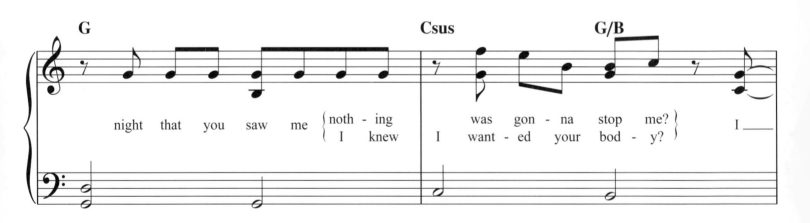

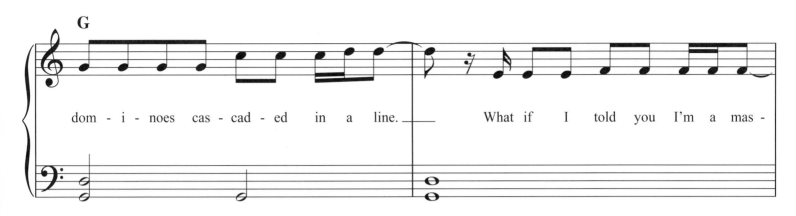

dom - i - noes cas - cad - ed in a line. ___ What if I told you I'm a mas-

- ter - mind? And now you're mine. ___

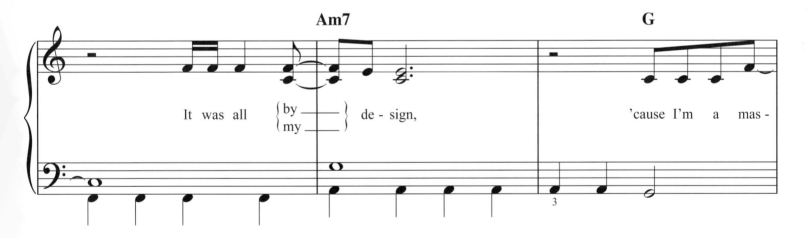

It was all {by ___ / my ___} de - sign, 'cause I'm a mas-

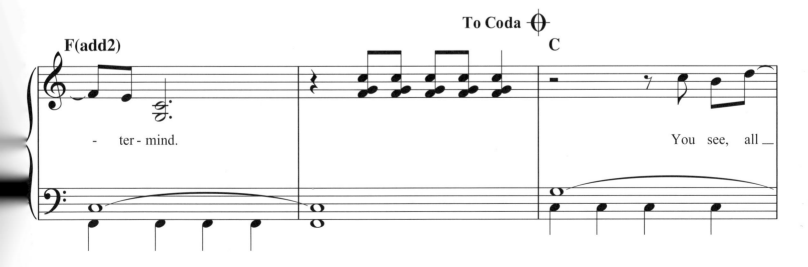

- ter - mind. You see, all ___

48

the wis - est wom - en had to do it this way, ___

'cause we were born to be ___ the pawn ___ in ev - 'ry

lov - er's game. _ If you fail ___ to plan, you ___ plan to fail.

___ Strat - e - gy ___ sets the scene _ for the tale. ___ I'm the wind _

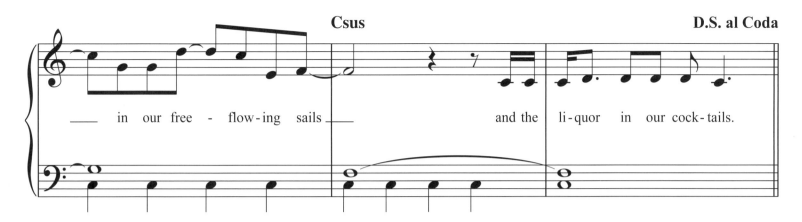

Csus   **D.S. al Coda**

_____ in our free - flow-ing sails _____ and the li-quor in our cock-tails.

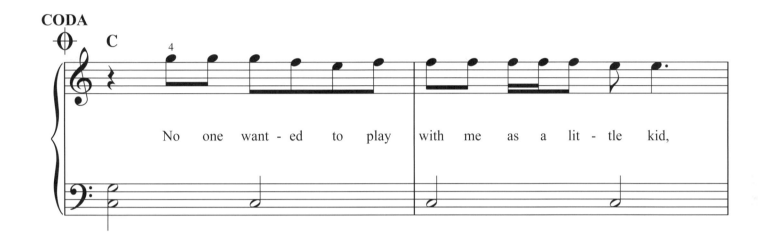

CODA   **C**

No one want-ed to play with me as a lit-tle kid,

C/F

so I've been schem-ing like a crim-i-nal ev-er since, to make them love me and

make it seem ef-fort-less. This is the first___ time I've felt the need___ to con-fess, and

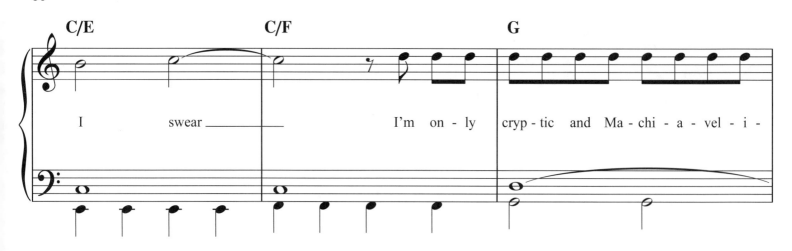

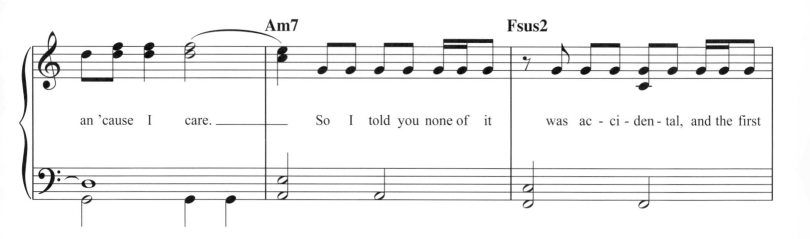

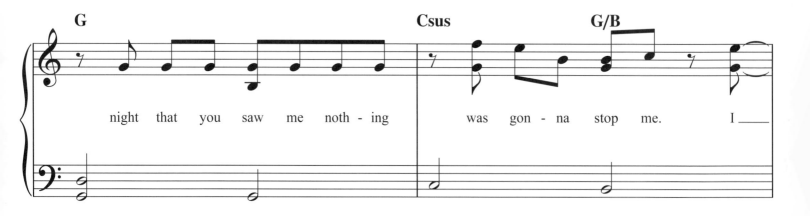

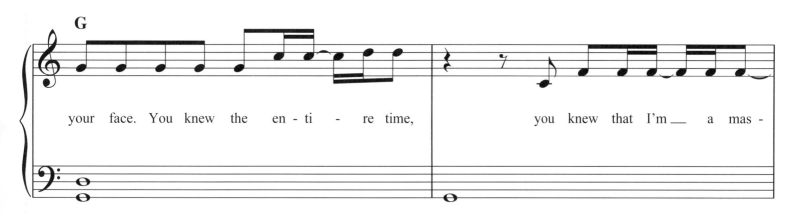

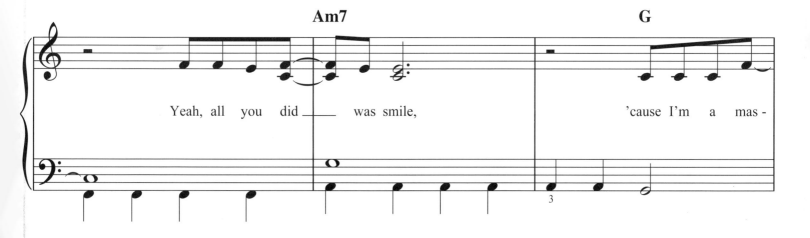

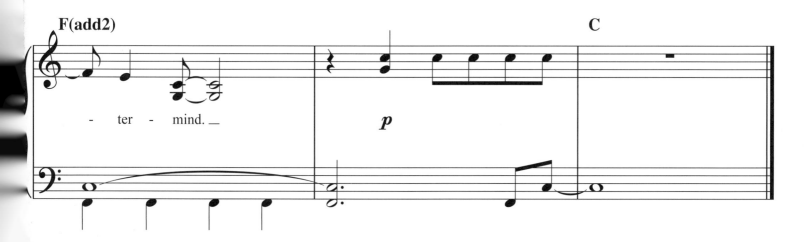

QUESTION...?

Words and Music by TAYLOR SWIFT
and JACK ANTONOFF

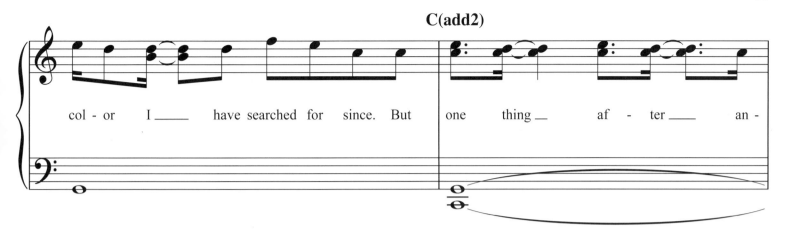

C(add2)

col - or I ___ have searched for since. But one thing ___ af - ter ___ an -

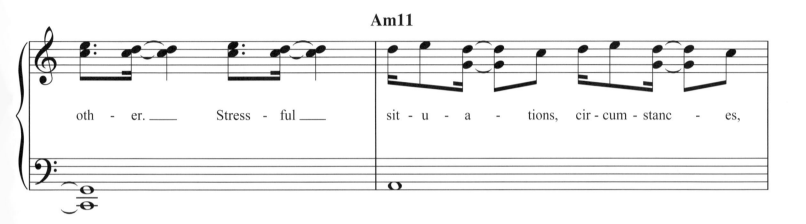

Am11

oth - er. ___ Stress - ful ___ sit - u - a - tions, cir - cum - stanc - es,

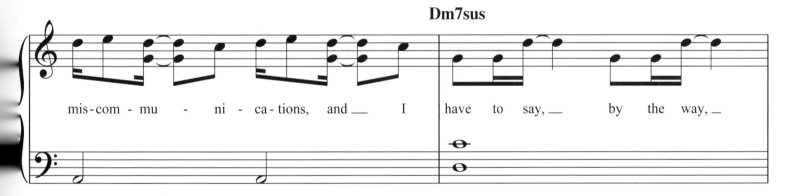

Dm7sus

mis - com - mu - ni - ca - tions, and ___ I have to say, ___ by the way, ___

Gsus

I just may ___ like some ex - pla - na - tions. Can I ask you a ques-

54

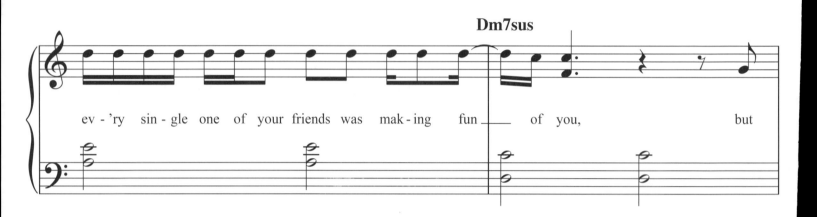

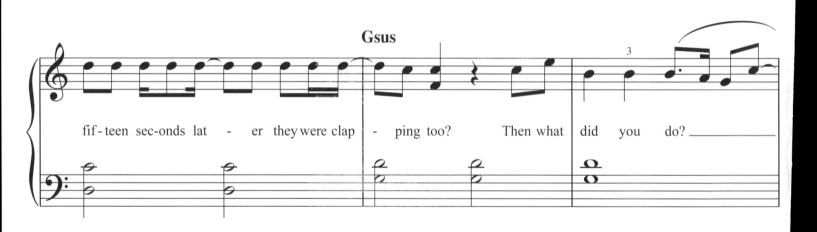

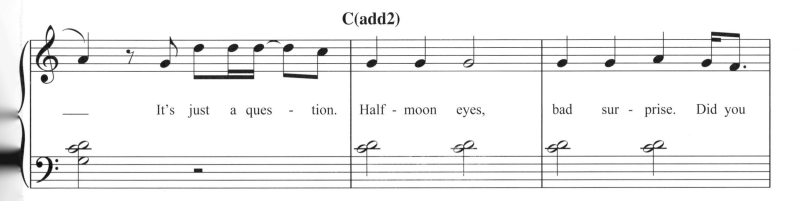

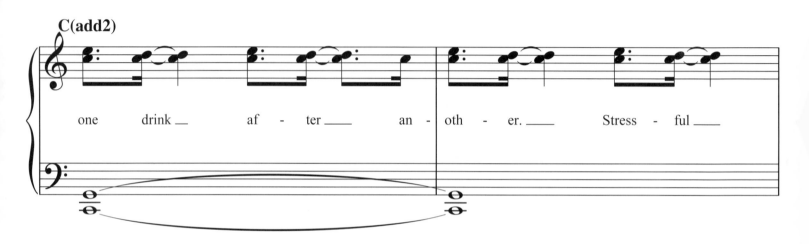

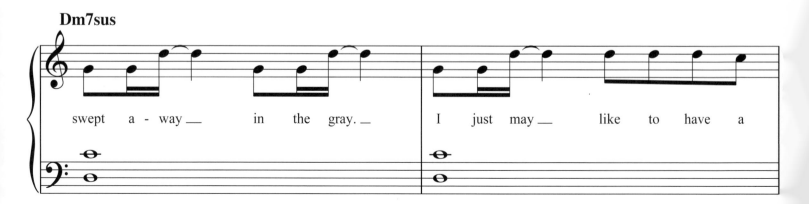

Gsus

con - ver - sa - tion.　　Can I ask you a ques-

C(add2)

-tion?　　Did you ev - er have some - one kiss you in ____ a crowd-

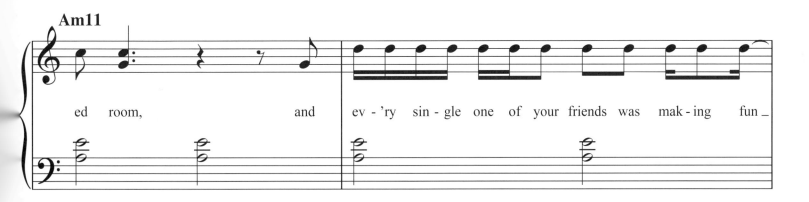

Am11

ed room,　　and ev - 'ry sin - gle one of your friends was mak - ing fun __

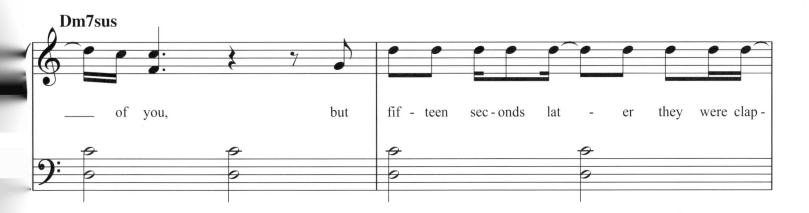

Dm7sus

__ of you,　　but fif - teen sec - onds lat - er they were clap-

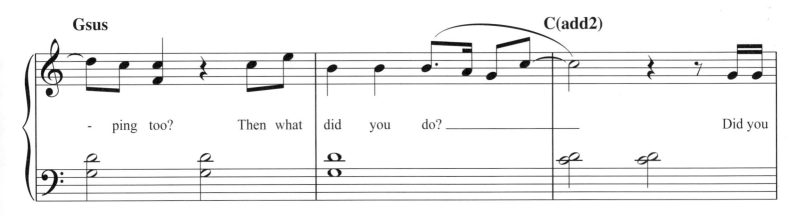

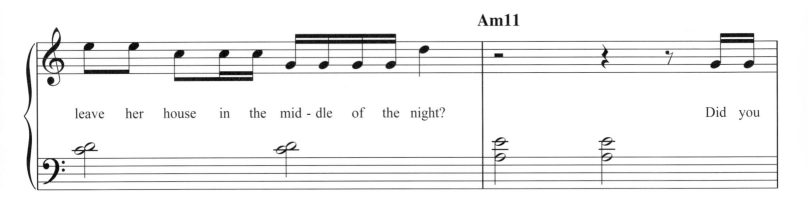

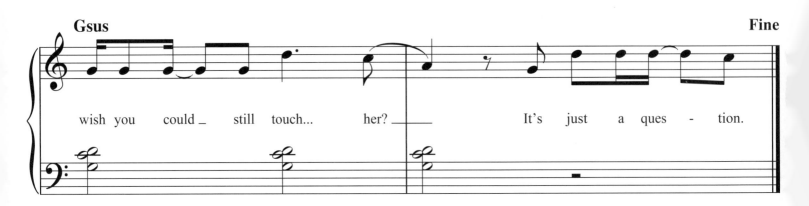

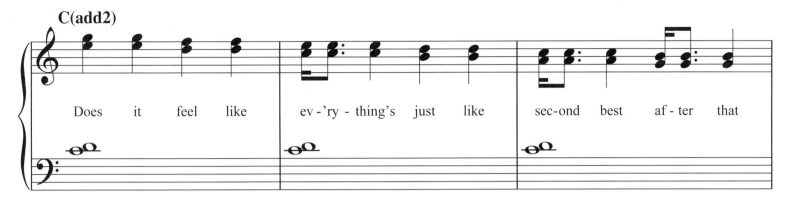

C(add2)

Does it feel like ev-'ry - thing's just like sec-ond best af - ter that

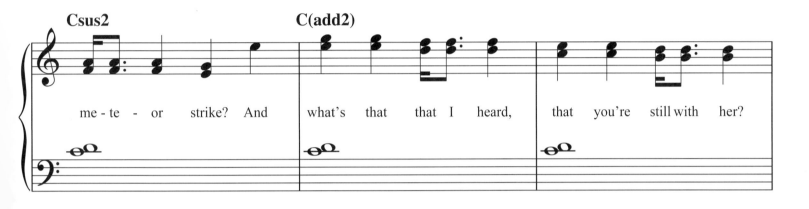

Csus2   **C(add2)**

me - te - or strike? And what's that that I heard, that you're still with her?

Csus2   **C(add2)**

That's nice. I'm sure that's what's suit - a - ble _____ and

Csus2   **D.S. al Fine**

right. _____ But to - night, _____ can I ask you a ques-

VIGILANTE S***

Words and Music by
TAYLOR SWIFT

Draw the cat eye sharp e-nough to kill a man.

You did some bad things but I'm the worst of them.

Some-times I won-der which one will be your last lie.

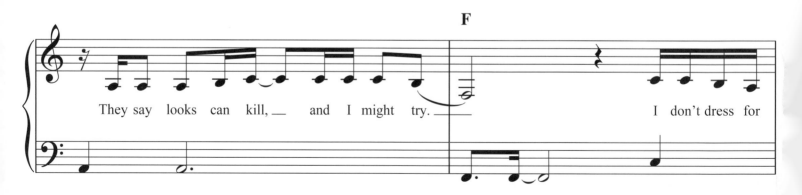

They say looks can kill, __ and I might try. __ I don't dress for

wom - en, I don't dress for men: late - ly I've been dress - ing for re -

venge. _ I don't start it, but I can tell you how it

ends: _ don't get sad, get e - ven. _ So on the week-

ends I don't dress for friends: late - ly I've been dress - ing for re - venge. _

She need-ed cold, hard proof, so I gave her some.

She had the en-ve-lope, where you think she got it from?

Now she gets the house, gets the kids, gets the pride.

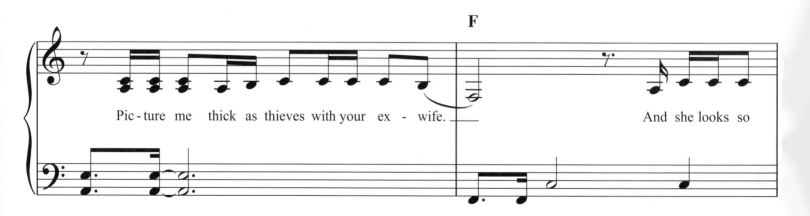

Pic-ture me thick as thieves with your ex - wife. And she looks so

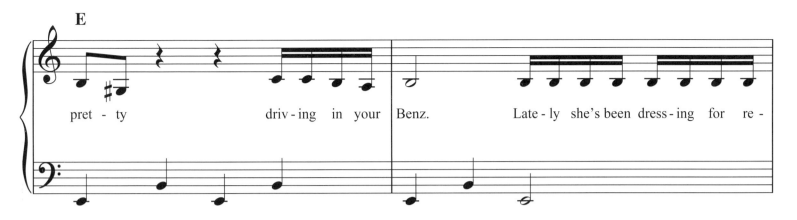

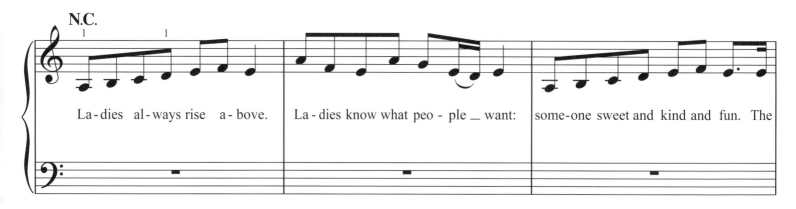

Ladies al-ways rise a-bove. La-dies know what peo-ple — want: some-one sweet and kind and fun. The

la — dy simp-ly had e — nough. — While he was do-ing

lines — and cross-ing all of mine, — some-one told his white col-lar

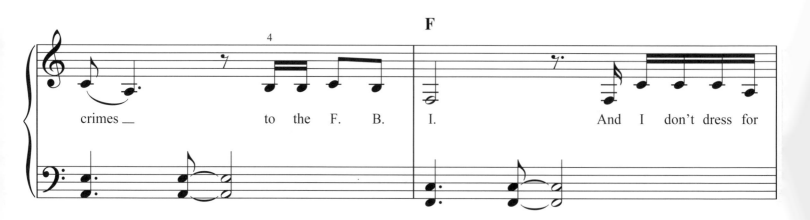

crimes — to the F. B. I. And I don't dress for

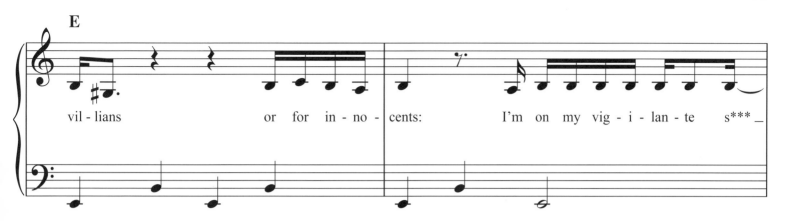

vil - lians   or   for   in - no - cents: I'm   on   my   vig - i - lan - te   s***_

_____   a - gain. ___   I   don't   start   it,   but   I   can   tell   you   how   it

ends: _____   don't   get   sad,   get   e - ven. ___   So   on   the   week-

ends   I   don't   dress   for   friends: late-ly   I've   been   dress-ing   for   re   - venge. _

BEJEWELED

Words and Music by TAYLOR SWIFT
and JACK ANTONOFF

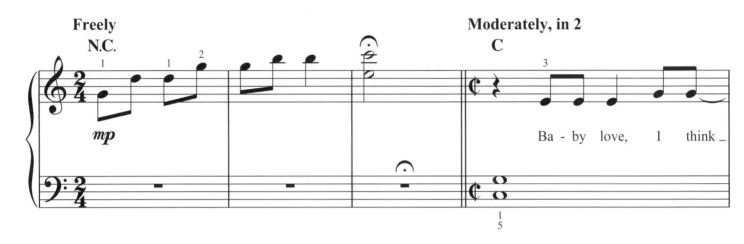

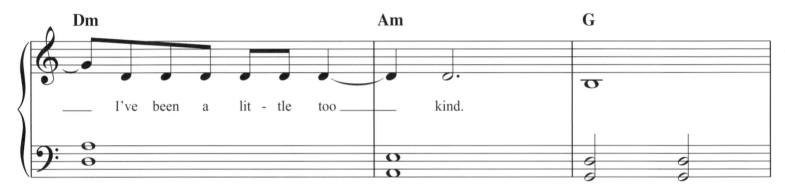

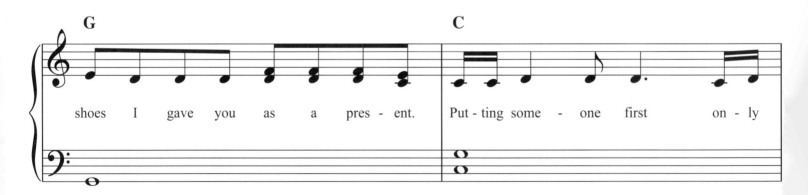

works when you're in their top ____ five. ____ And by the

way, ____ I'm go - ing out to - night.

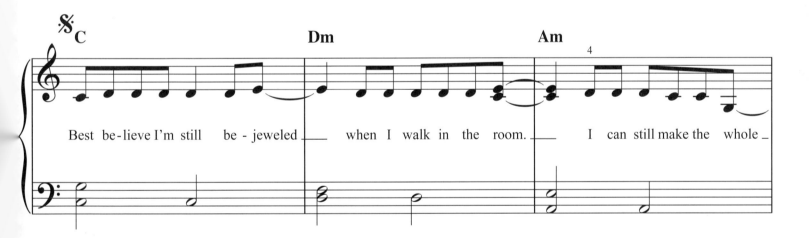

Best be - lieve I'm still be - jeweled ____ when I walk in the room. ____ I can still make the whole ____

____ place shim - mer. And when I meet the band, ____ they ask, "Do you have a man?" ____

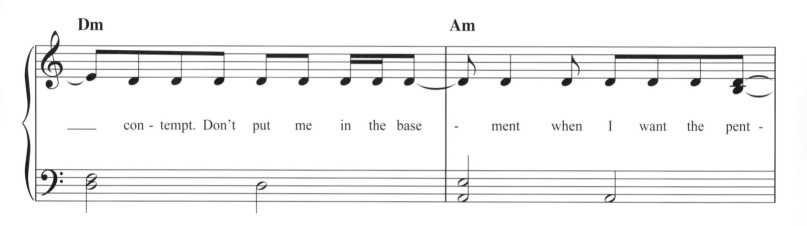

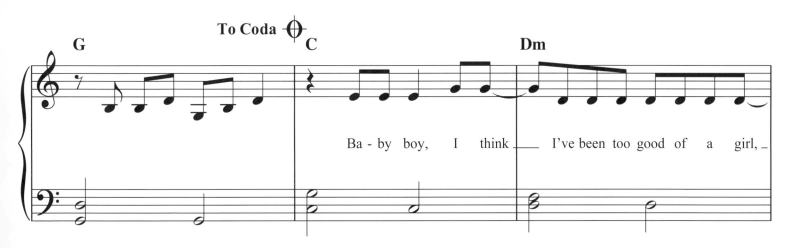

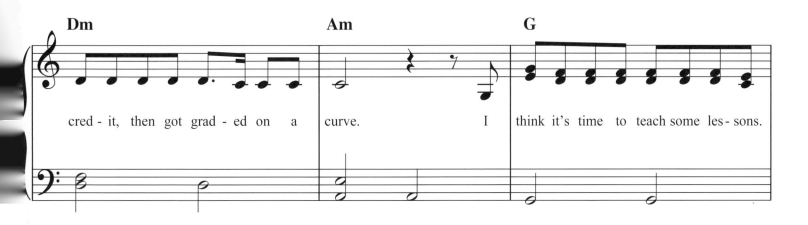

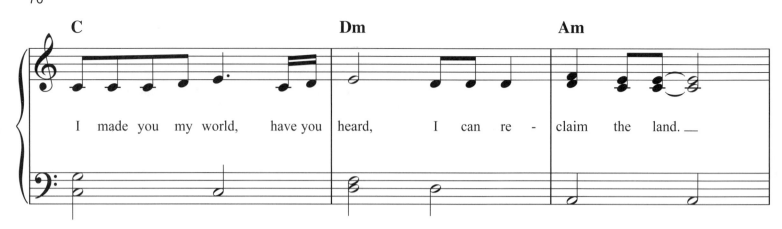

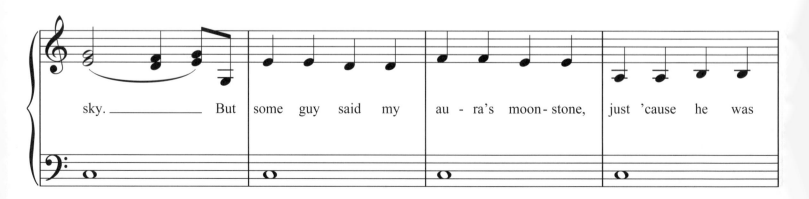

high. _____ We're danc-ing all night _ and you can try

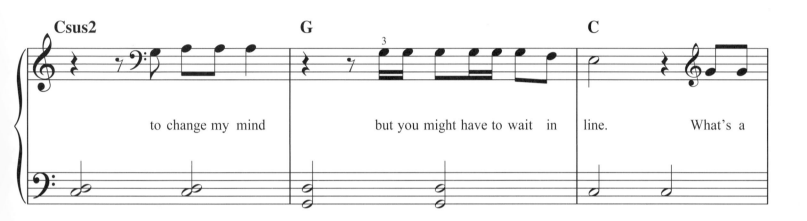

to change my mind but you might have to wait in line. What's a

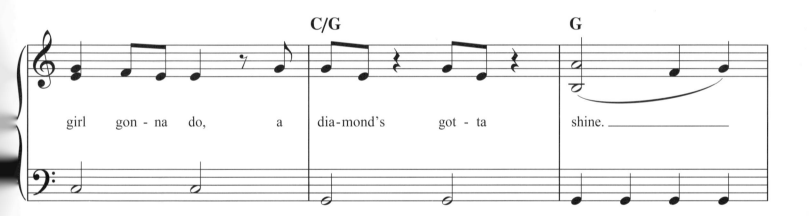

girl gon - na do, a dia-mond's got - ta shine. _____

Best be-lieve I'm still be - jeweled _ when I walk in the room. _ I can still make the whole _

place shim-mer. And when I meet the band,___ they ask, "Do you have a man?"_

___ I could still say, "I don't___ re - mem-ber." Fa - mil - i - ar - i - ty breeds_

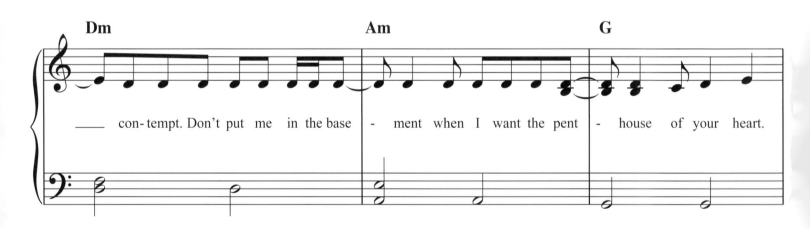

___ con - tempt. Don't put me in the base - ment when I want the pent - house of your heart.

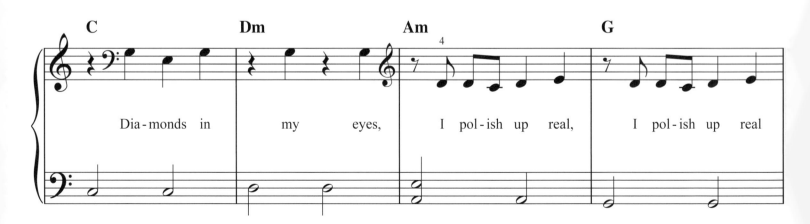

Dia-monds in my eyes, I pol-ish up real, I pol-ish up real

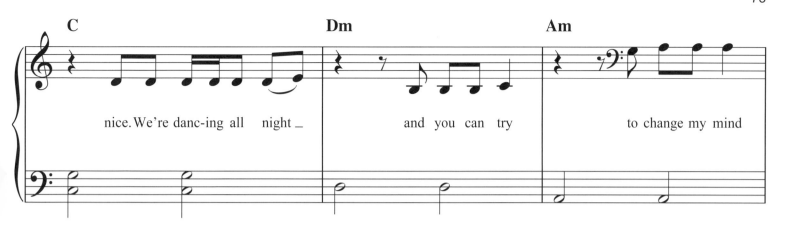

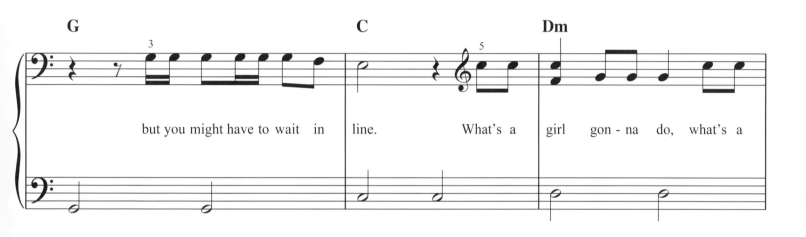

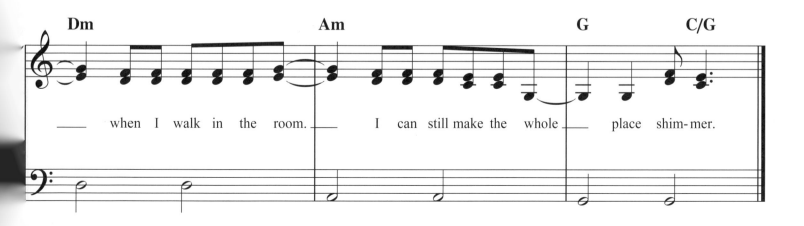

LABYRINTH

Words and Music by TAYLOR SWIFT
and JACK ANTONOFF

Atmospheric Pop

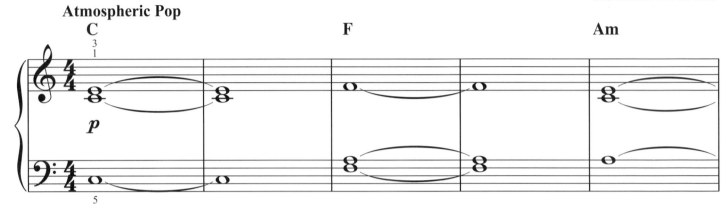

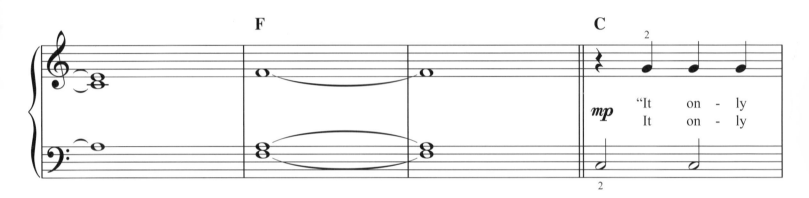

"It on - ly
It on - ly

hurts this ___ much | right ___ now" | was what I was
feels this ___ raw | right ___ now, | lost in the lab -

think - ing | the whole ___ time.
y - rinth | of my ___ mind.

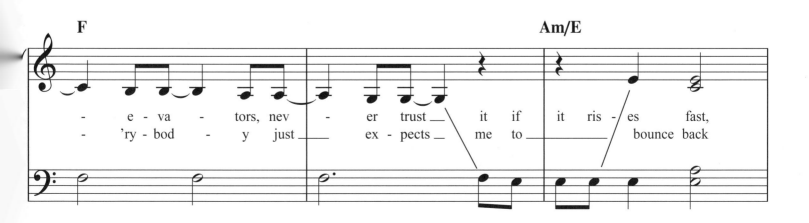

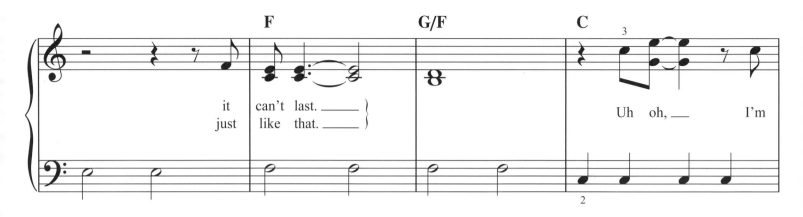

it can't last. _____
just like that. _____

Uh oh, ___ I'm

fall-ing in love. ___

Oh no, ___ I'm fall-ing in love a-gain. ___

___ Oh, ___ I'm fall-ing in love. I thought the plane was go-ing down.

How'd you turn it right a-round?

Uh oh, ___ I'm fall-ing in love. ___

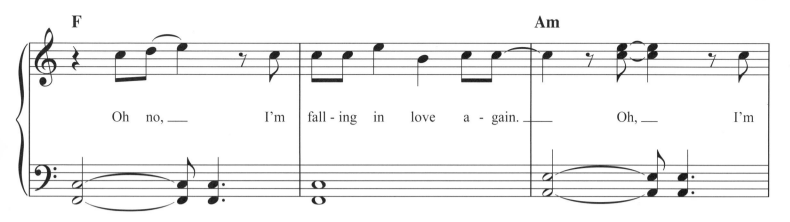

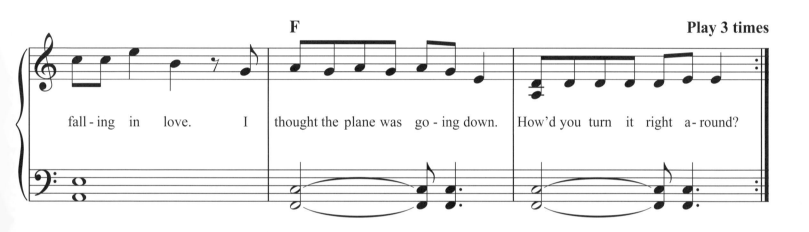

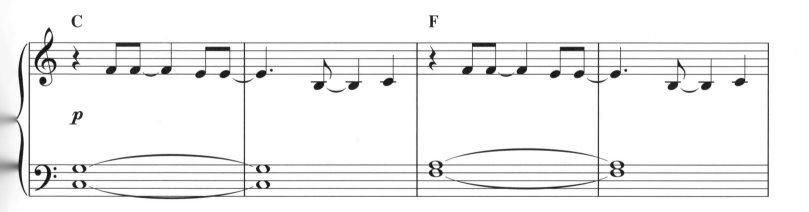

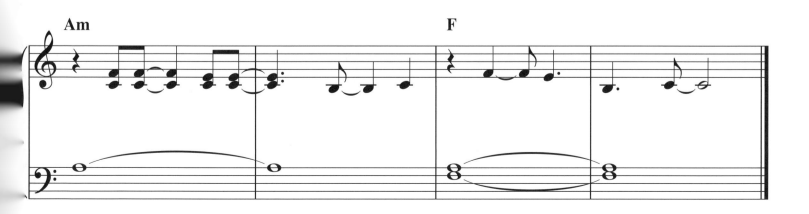

SWEET NOTHING

Words and Music by TAYLOR SWIFT
and WILLIAM BOWERY

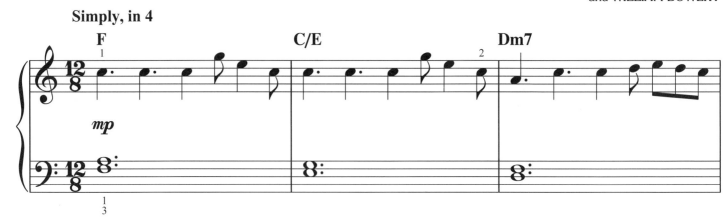

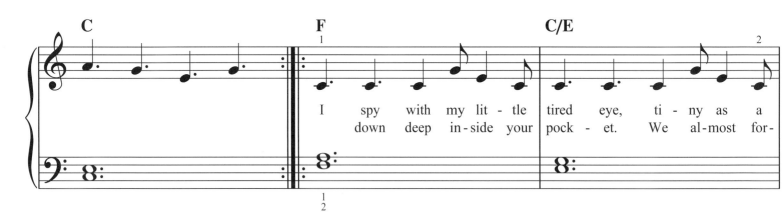

I spy with my lit - tle tired eye, ti - ny as a
down deep in - side your pock - et. We al - most for-

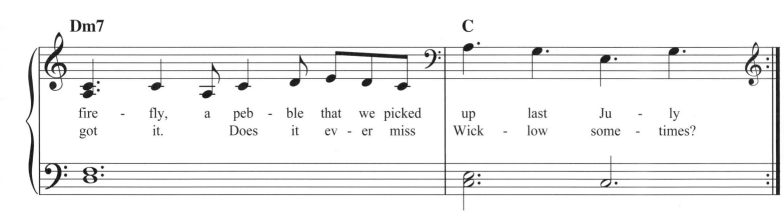

fire - fly, a peb - ble that we picked up last Ju - ly
got it. Does it ev - er miss Wick - low some - times?

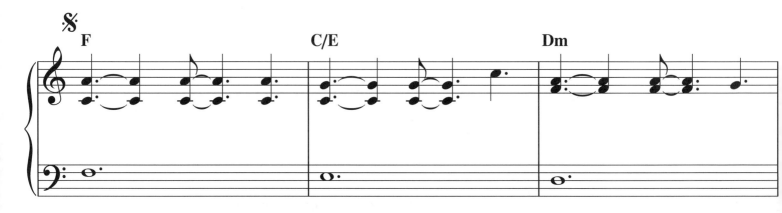

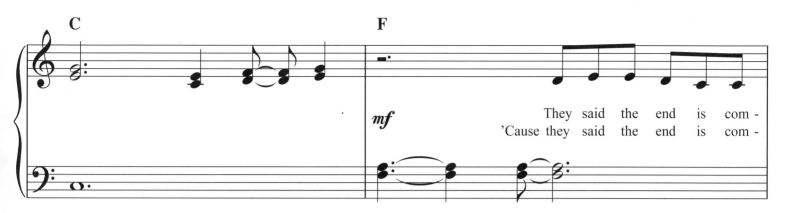

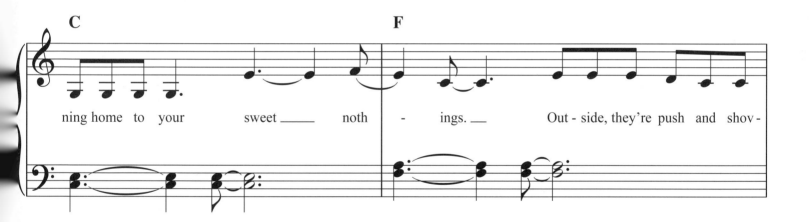

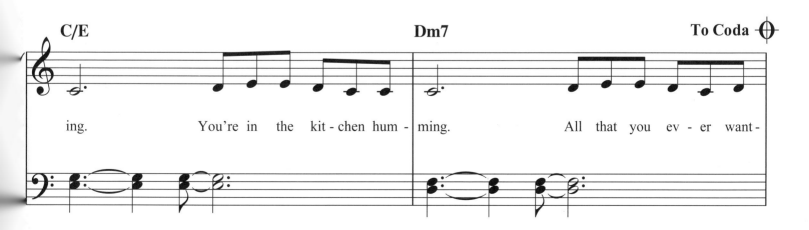

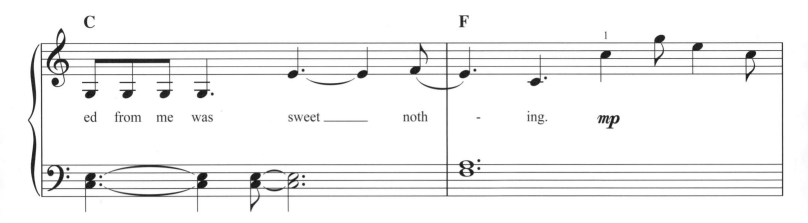

ed from me was sweet _____ noth - ing. *mp*

On the way home   I wrote a poem.   You say, "What a mind!"

D.S. al Coda

CODA

This hap - pens all the time.

ed from me was noth - ing. ___

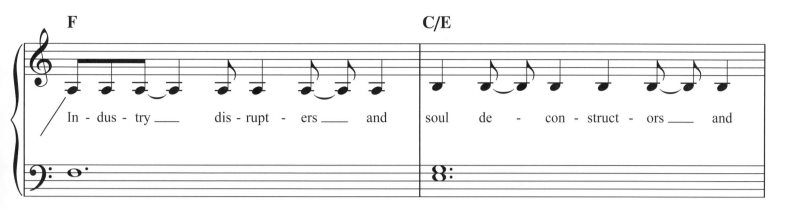

In - dus - try ___ dis - rupt - ers ___ and soul de - con - struct - ors ___ and

smooth talk - ing huck - sters ___ out glad - hand - ing each oth - er ___ and the

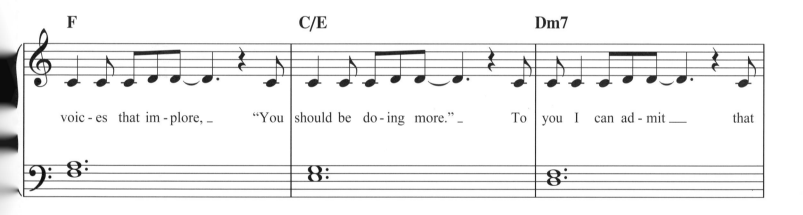

voic - es that im - plore, ___ "You should be do - ing more." ___ To you I can ad - mit ___ that

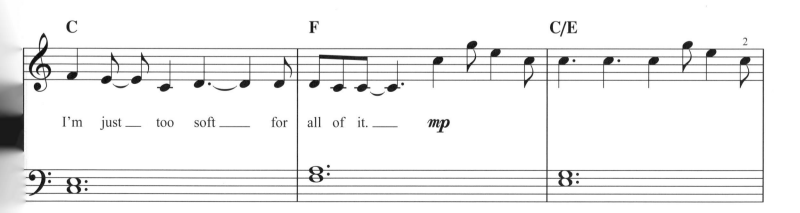

I'm just ___ too soft ___ for all of it. ___ *mp*

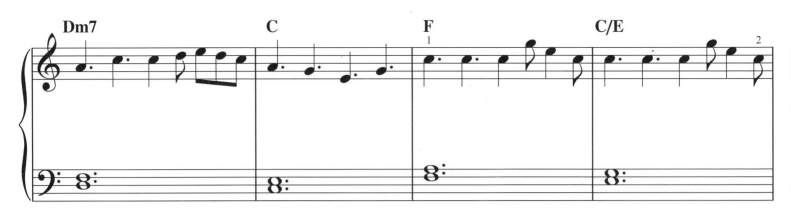

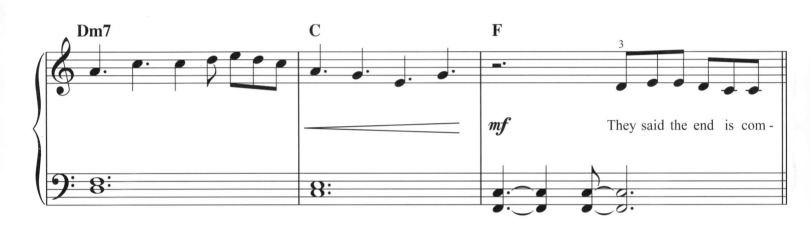

They said the end is com-

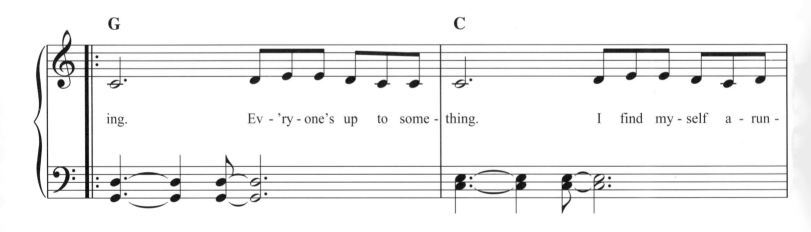

ing. Ev-'ry-one's up to some-thing. I find my-self a-run-

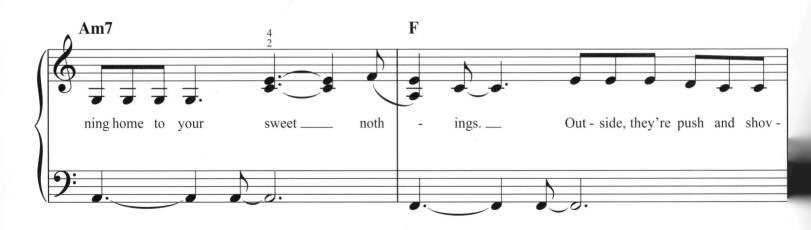

ning home to your sweet ____ noth - ings. ____ Out - side, they're push and shov-

MIDNIGHT RAIN

Words and Music by TAYLOR SWIFT
and JACK ANTONOFF

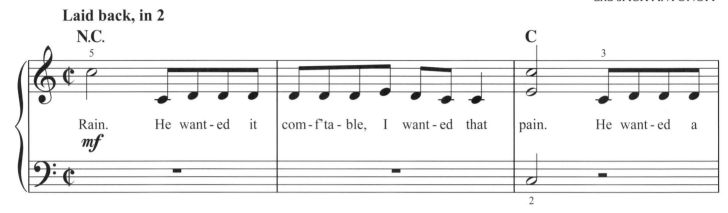

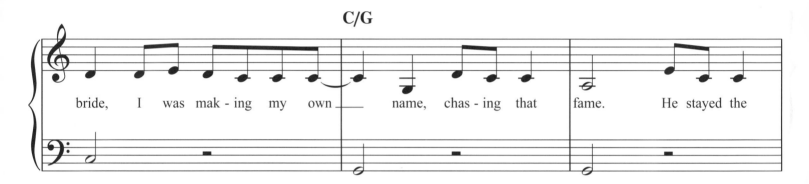

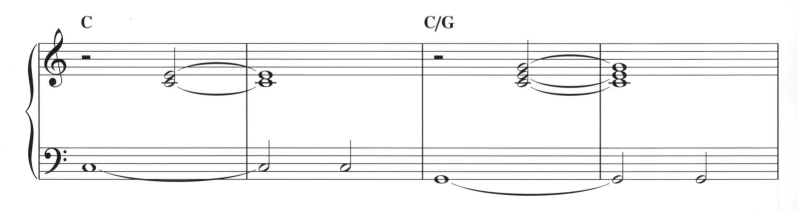

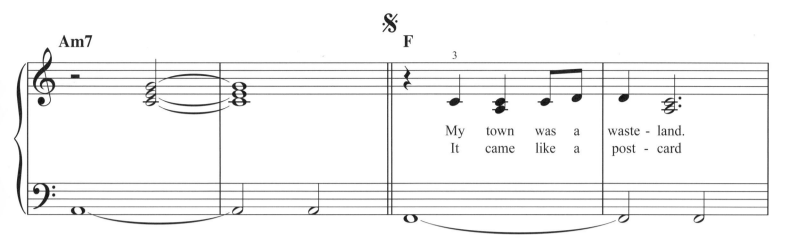

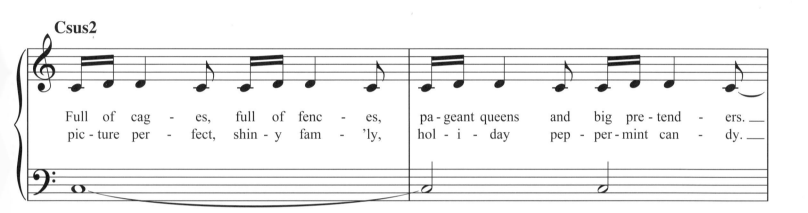

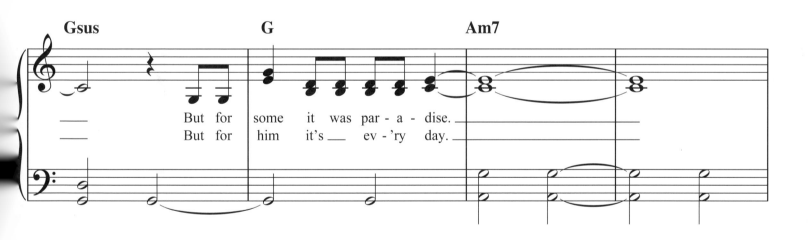

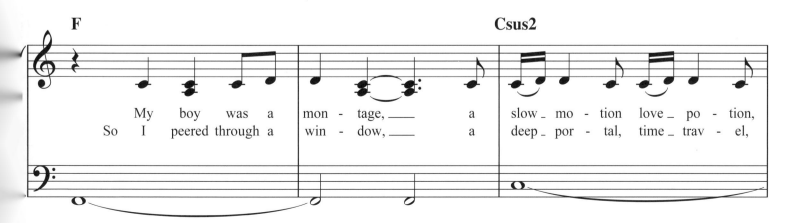

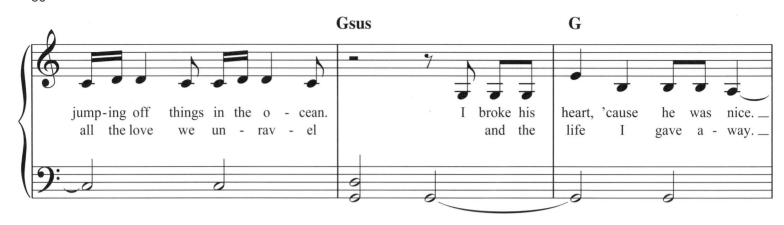

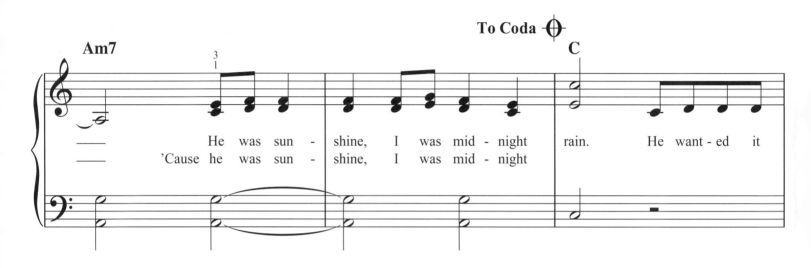

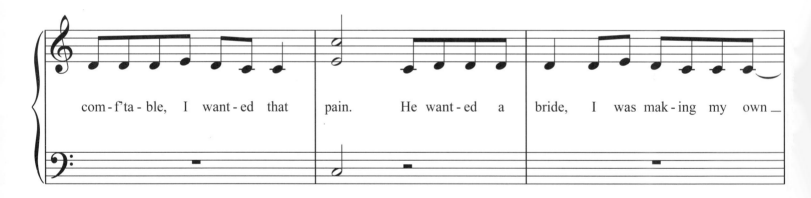

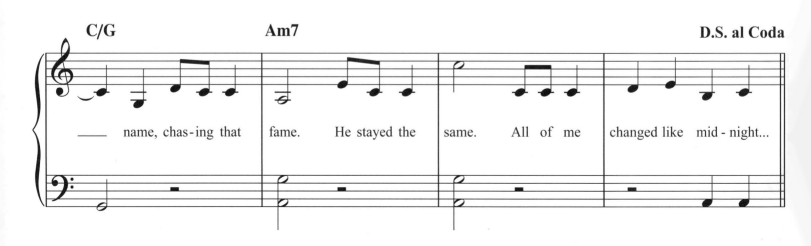

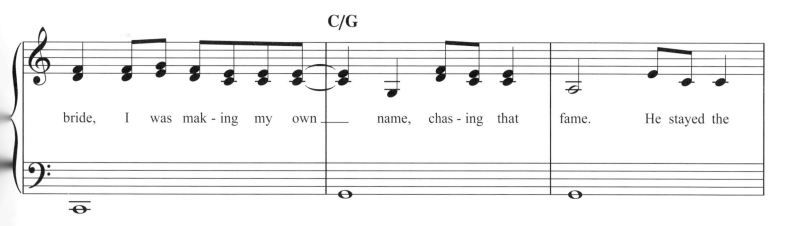

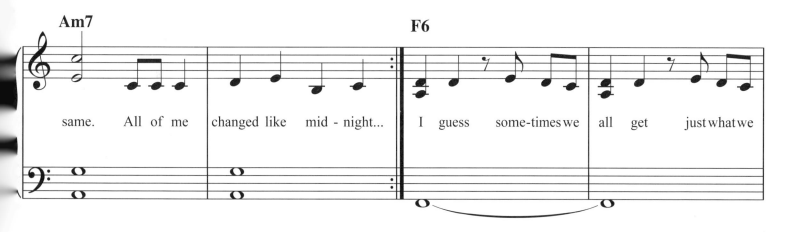

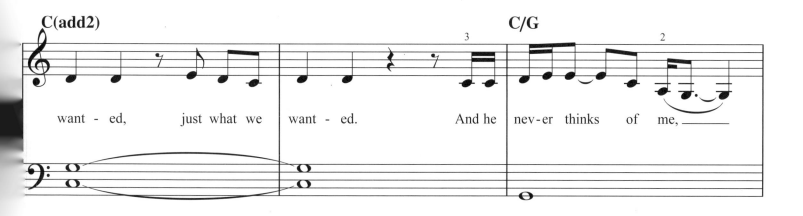

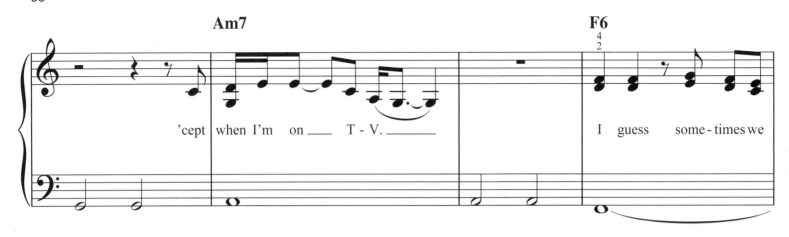

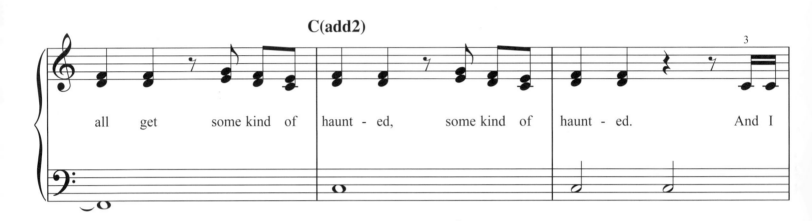

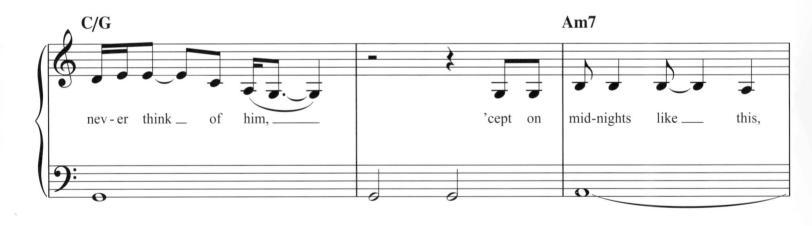

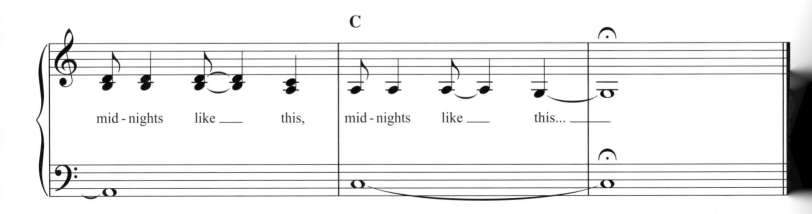